LEONID BREZHNEV

LEONID BREZHNEV

Ina L. Navazelskis

CHELSEA HOUSE PUBLISHERS
NEW YORK
NEW HAVEN   PHILADELPHIA

EDITOR-IN-CHIEF: Nancy Toff
EXECUTIVE EDITOR: Remmel T. Nunn
MANAGING EDITOR: Karyn Gullen Browne
COPY CHIEF: Juliann Barbato
ART DIRECTOR: Giannella Garrett
MANUFACTURING MANAGER: Gerald Levine

Staff for BREZHNEV:

SENIOR EDITOR: John W. Selfridge
ASSISTANT EDITORS: Pierre Hauser, Kathleen McDermott, Bert Yaeger
EDITORIAL ASSISTANT: James Guiry
COPY EDITORS: Gillian Bucky, Sean Dolan, Ellen Scordato, Michael Goodman
PICTURE EDITOR: Juliette Dickstein
DESIGN ASSISTANT: Jill Goldreyer
PICTURE RESEARCH: Karen Herman
LAYOUT: Teresa Clark
PRODUCTION COORDINATOR: Laura McCormick
COVER ILLUSTRATION: Kye Carbone

CREATIVE DIRECTOR: Harold Steinberg

Frontispiece courtesy of TASS from SOVFOTO

3 5 7 9 8 6 4 2

Library of Congress Cataloging in Publication Data

Navazelskis, Ina. LEONID BREZHNEV

(World leaders past & present)
Bibliography: p.
Includes index.
1. Brezhnev, Leonid Ilích, 1906–1982— Juvenile literature.
2. Heads of state—Soviet Union—Biography— Juvenile
literature. 3. Soviet Union—Presidents—Biography—
Juvenile literature. [1. Brezhnev, Leonid Ilích, 1906–1982.
3. Heads of state] I. Title. II. Series: World leaders past &
present.
DK275.B7N38   1987   947.085'3'0924 [B] [92]   87-9358

ISBN 0-87754-513-8

Contents

CHELSEA HOUSE PUBLISHERS

WORLD LEADERS PAST & PRESENT

ADENAUER	FREDERICK THE GREAT	MARY, QUEEN OF SCOTS
ALEXANDER THE GREAT	INDIRA GANDHI	GOLDA MEIR
MARC ANTONY	MOHANDAS GANDHI	METTERNICH
KING ARTHUR	GARIBALDI	MUSSOLINI
ATATÜRK	GENGHIS KHAN	NAPOLEON
ATTLEE	GLADSTONE	NASSER
BEGIN	GORBACHEV	NEHRU
BEN-GURION	HAMMARSKJÖLD	NERO
BISMARCK	HENRY VIII	NICHOLAS II
LÉON BLUM	HENRY OF NAVARRE	NIXON
BOLÍVAR	HINDENBURG	NKRUMAH
CESARE BORGIA	HITLER	PERICLES
BRANDT	HO CHI MINH	PERÓN
BREZHNEV	HUSSEIN	QADDAFI
CAESAR	IVAN THE TERRIBLE	ROBESPIERRE
CALVIN	ANDREW JACKSON	ELEANOR ROOSEVELT
CASTRO	JEFFERSON	FRANKLIN D. ROOSEVELT
CATHERINE THE GREAT	JOAN OF ARC	THEODORE ROOSEVELT
CHARLEMAGNE	POPE JOHN XXIII	SADAT
CHIANG KAI-SHEK	LYNDON JOHNSON	STALIN
CHURCHILL	JUÁREZ	SUN YAT-SEN
CLEMENCEAU	JOHN F. KENNEDY	TAMERLANE
CLEOPATRA	KENYATTA	THATCHER
CORTÉS	KHOMEINI	TITO
CROMWELL	KHRUSHCHEV	TROTSKY
DANTON	MARTIN LUTHER KING, JR.	TRUDEAU
DE GAULLE	KISSINGER	TRUMAN
DE VALERA	LENIN	VICTORIA
DISRAELI	LINCOLN	WASHINGTON
EISENHOWER	LLOYD GEORGE	WEIZMANN
ELEANOR OF AQUITAINE	LOUIS XIV	WOODROW WILSON
QUEEN ELIZABETH I	LUTHER	XERXES
FERDINAND AND ISABELLA	JUDAS MACCABEUS	ZHOU ENLAI
FRANCO	MAO ZEDONG	

ON LEADERSHIP
Arthur M. Schlesinger, jr.

LEADERSHIP, it may be said, is really what makes the world go round. Love no doubt smooths the passage; but love is a private transaction between consenting adults. Leadership is a public transaction with history. The idea of leadership affirms the capacity of individuals to move, inspire, and mobilize masses of people so that they act together in pursuit of an end. Sometimes leadership serves good purposes, sometimes bad; but whether the end is benign or evil, great leaders are those men and women who leave their personal stamp on history.

Now, the very concept of leadership implies the proposition that individuals can make a difference. This proposition has never been universally accepted. From classical times to the present day, eminent thinkers have regarded individuals as no more than the agents and pawns of larger forces, whether the gods and goddesses of the ancient world or, in the modern era, race, class, nation, the dialectic, the will of the people, the spirit of the times, history itself. Against such forces, the individual dwindles into insignificance.

So contends the thesis of historical determinism. Tolstoy's great novel *War and Peace* offers a famous statement of the case. Why, Tolstoy asked, did millions of men in the Napoleonic wars, denying their human feelings and their common sense, move back and forth across Europe slaughtering their fellows? "The war," Tolstoy answered, "was bound to happen simply because it was bound to happen." All prior history predetermined it. As for leaders, they, Tolstoy said, "are but the labels that serve to give a name to an end and, like labels, they have the least possible connection with the event." The greater the leader, "the more conspicuous the inevitability and the predestination of every act he commits." The leader, said Tolstoy, is "the slave of history."

Determinism takes many forms. Marxism is the determinism of class. Nazism the determinism of race. But the idea of men and women as the slaves of history runs athwart the deepest human instincts. Rigid determinism abolishes the idea of human freedom—

7

the assumption of free choice that underlies every move we make, every word we speak, every thought we think. It abolishes the idea of human responsibility, since it is manifestly unfair to reward or punish people for actions that are by definition beyond their control. No one can live consistently by any deterministic creed. The Marxist states prove this themselves by their extreme susceptibility to the cult of leadership.

More than that, history refutes the idea that individuals make no difference. In December 1931 a British politician crossing Park Avenue in New York City between 76th and 77th Streets around 10:30 P.M. looked in the wrong direction and was knocked down by an automobile—a moment, he later recalled, of a man aghast, a world aglare: "I do not understand why I was not broken like an eggshell or squashed like a gooseberry." Fourteen months later an American politician, sitting in an open car in Miami, Florida, was fired on by an assassin; the man beside him was hit. Those who believe that individuals make no difference to history might well ponder whether the next two decades would have been the same had Mario Constasino's car killed Winston Churchill in 1931 and Giuseppe Zangara's bullet killed Franklin Roosevelt in 1933. Suppose, in addition, that Adolf Hitler had been killed in the street fighting during the Munich *Putsch* of 1923 and that Lenin had died of typhus during World War I. What would the 20th century be like now?

For better or for worse, individuals do make a difference. "The notion that a people can run itself and its affairs anonymously," wrote the philosopher William James, "is now well known to be the silliest of absurdities. Mankind does nothing save through initiatives on the part of inventors, great or small, and imitation by the rest of us—these are the sole factors in human progress. Individuals of genius show the way, and set the patterns, which common people then adopt and follow."

Leadership, James suggests, means leadership in thought as well as in action. In the long run, leaders in thought may well make the greater difference to the world. But, as Woodrow Wilson once said, "Those only are leaders of men, in the general eye, who lead in action. . . . It is at their hands that new thought gets its translation into the crude language of deeds." Leaders in thought often invent in solitude and obscurity, leaving to later generations the tasks of imitation. Leaders in action—the leaders portrayed in this series—have to be effective in their own time.

And they cannot be effective by themselves. They must act in response to the rhythms of their age. Their genius must be adapted, in a phrase of William James's, "to the receptivities of the moment." Leaders are useless without followers. "There goes the mob," said the French politician hearing a clamor in the streets. "I am their leader. I must follow them." Great leaders turn the inchoate emotions of the mob to purposes of their own. They seize on the opportunities of their time, the hopes, fears, frustrations, crises, potentialities. They succeed when events have prepared the way for them, when the community is awaiting to be aroused, when they can provide the clarifying and organizing ideas. Leadership ignites the circuit between the individual and the mass and thereby alters history.

It may alter history for better or for worse. Leaders have been responsible for the most extravagant follies and most monstrous crimes that have beset suffering humanity. They have also been vital in such gains as humanity has made in individual freedom, religious and racial tolerance, social justice and respect for human rights.

There is no sure way to tell in advance who is going to lead for good and who for evil. But a glance at the gallery of men and women in *World Leaders—Past and Present* suggests some useful tests.

One test is this: do leaders lead by force or by persuasion? By command or by consent? Through most of history leadership was exercised by the divine right of authority. The duty of followers was to defer and to obey. "Theirs not to reason why,/ Theirs but to do and die." On occasion, as with the so-called "enlightened despots" of the 18th century in Europe, absolutist leadership was animated by humane purposes. More often, absolutism nourished the passion for domination, land, gold and conquest and resulted in tyranny.

The great revolution of modern times has been the revolution of equality. The idea that all people should be equal in their legal condition has undermined the old structure of authority, hierarchy and deference. The revolution of equality has had two contrary effects on the nature of leadership. For equality, as Alexis de Tocqueville pointed out in his great study *Democracy in America*, might mean equality in servitude as well as equality in freedom.

"I know of only two methods of establishing equality in the political world," Tocqueville wrote. "Rights must be given to every citizen, or none at all to anyone . . . save one, who is the master of all." There was no middle ground "between the sovereignty of all and the absolute power of one man." In his astonishing prediction of 20th-century totalitarian dictatorship, Tocqueville explained how the revolution of equality could lead to the *"Führerprinzip"* and more terrible absolutism than the world had ever known.

But when rights are given to every citizen and the sovereignty of all is established, the problem of leadership takes a new form, becomes more exacting than ever before. It is easy to issue commands and enforce them by the rope and the stake, the concentration camp and the *gulag.* It is much harder to use argument and achievement to overcome opposition and win consent. The Founding Fathers of the United States understood the difficulty. They believed that history had given them the opportunity to decide, as Alexander Hamilton wrote in the first Federalist Paper, whether men are indeed capable of basing government on "reflection and choice, or whether they are forever destined to depend . . . on accident and force."

Government by reflection and choice called for a new style of leadership and a new quality of followership. It required leaders to be responsive to popular concerns, and it required followers to be active and informed participants in the process. Democracy does not eliminate emotion from politics; sometimes it fosters demagoguery; but it is confident that, as the greatest of democratic leaders put it, you cannot fool all of the people all of the time. It measures leadership by results and retires those who overreach or falter or fail.

It is true that in the long run despots are measured by results too. But they can postpone the day of judgment, sometimes indefinitely, and in the meantime they can do infinite harm. It is also true that democracy is no guarantee of virtue and intelligence in government, for the voice of the people is not necessarily the voice of God. But democracy, by assuring the right of opposition, offers built-in resistance to the evils inherent in absolutism. As the theologian Reinhold Niebuhr summed it up, "Man's capacity for justice makes democracy possible, but man's inclination to injustice makes democracy necessary."

A second test for leadership is the end for which power is sought. When leaders have as their goal the supremacy of a master race or the promotion of totalitarian revolution or the acquisition and exploitation of colonies or the protection of greed and privilege or the preservation of personal power, it is likely that their leadership will do little to advance the cause of humanity. When their goal is the abolition of slavery, the liberation of women, the enlargement of opportunity for the poor and powerless, the extension of equal rights to racial minorities, the defense of the freedoms of expression and opposition, it is likely that their leadership will increase the sum of human liberty and welfare.

Leaders have done great harm to the world. They have also conferred great benefits. You will find both sorts in this series. Even "good" leaders must be regarded with a certain wariness. Leaders are not demigods; they put on their trousers one leg after another just like ordinary mortals. No leader is infallible, and every leader needs to be reminded of this at regular intervals. Irreverence irritates leaders but is their salvation. Unquestioning submission corrupts leaders and demands followers. Making a cult of a leader is always a mistake. Fortunately hero worship generates its own antidote. "Every hero," said Emerson, "becomes a bore at last."

The signal benefit the great leaders confer is to embolden the rest of us to live according to our own best selves, to be active, insistent, and resolute in affirming our own sense of things. For great leaders attest to the reality of human freedom against the supposed inevitabilities of history. And they attest to the wisdom and power that may lie within the most unlikely of us, which is why Abraham Lincoln remains the supreme example of great leadership. A great leader, said Emerson, exhibits new possibilities to all humanity. "We feed on genius. . . . Great men exist that there may be greater men."

Great leaders, in short, justify themselves by emancipating and empowering their followers. So humanity struggles to master its destiny, remembering with Alexis de Tocqueville: "It is true that around every man a fatal circle is traced beyond which he cannot pass; but within the wide verge of that circle he is powerful and free; as it is with man, so with communities."

1

In the Shadow of the Steel Mill

The head of the largest workers' state in the world — the society in which everyone is supposed to be equal — enjoyed a very privileged life-style. Leonid Ilich Brezhnev, general secretary of the Communist party of the Soviet Union and leader of the country, had an apartment in Moscow and a suburban bungalow in a special compound reserved for the highest government officials. He maintained a luxurious summer home, with an Olympic-sized swimming pool and a yacht, in the warm, sunny Crimea. He sported well-tailored Western suits and delighted in collecting the latest electronic gadgets. His passion for automobiles was widely known. In a country where only three percent of the population owned an automobile and the average citizen often waited

Had it not been for the Revolution Leonid Brezhnev might have become little more than a skilled worker.
—JOHN DORNBERG
Brezhnev biographer

With banners held high, supporters of the Bolshevik party march through Moscow. The political order imposed on Russia in 1917 by the Communists proved very beneficial to Leonid Brezhnev because it provided loyal party members with opportunities for rapid advancement.

13

years before he could buy one, Brezhnev owned several expensive imports.

Leonid Brezhnev had not always lived so well. He was born into a poor, working-class family on December 19, 1906, in the industrial town now called Dneprodzerzhinsk in the southern Ukraine. Kamenskoye, as the town was known until 1936, was a small and relatively new settlement at the turn of the century. It was a frontier town that grew up around the Dneprovsky steel factory built there in the 1880s by the South Russian Metallurgical Company.

Kamenskoye was a mosaic of different nationalities and ethnic groups. Russians predominated in the town itself, but in the surrounding countryside Ukrainian farmers made up the overwhelming majority. The steel factory was owned by a French-Belgian consortium, and the company's upper management and engineers were most often of Polish or German origin. There were also Czechs, Jews, Bulgarians, Greeks, Serbs, Tatars, and Moldavians in Kamenskoye.

The Brezhnev family, who were Russians, had settled in the Ukraine shortly after the Dneprovsky factory was built. They had been steelworkers for four generations — Leonid Brezhnev represented the fifth.

Brezhnev was the second of three children. He had an older sister, Vera, and a younger brother, born in 1908, named Yakov. Brezhnev's mother, Natalya, was a determined, deeply religious woman. Icons hung in the window of the Brezhnev home, a one-room house with a dirt floor, and the family regularly attended Russian Orthodox services. Because Ilya, Brezhnev's father, worked up to 18 hours in the steel mill each day, Natalya Brezhnev was the dominant influence at home. She was ambitious for her son Leonid, and she hoped he would become a skilled worker at the steel factory where his father worked. Mill foremen and the skilled laborers in Kamenskoye lived in the "Lower Colony," in neat cottages with individual garden plots, electricity, and

We did not trust him. We felt he was the kind who might do something behind your back.
—NATHAN KRUGLAK
classmate of Brezhnev

14

TASS FROM SOVFOTO

running water, which seemed to Natalya a wonderful improvement over the Brezhnev hovel.

It was therefore important that Leonid attend high school. The boys' high school, the *klassicheskaya gimnaziya*, required that prospective students pass examinations for reading, writing, and arithmetic. A tutor, therefore, had to be engaged to teach Leonid these skills. For a poor family, saving enough money to pay the tutor was no easy task. Still, they managed; Brezhnev passed the entrance exams and was accepted into the klassicheskaya gimnaziya in September 1915. The school was partly subsidized by the Dneprovsky steel factory, but the annual tuition was high — at least one month's wages for a steelworker.

This 1930 Brezhnev family portrait shows Leonid (top left) standing next to his wife, Viktoriya. The Brezhnev family was extremely poor prior to the Russian Revolution. Natalya Brezhnev (seated center) hoped that her eldest son, a fifth-generation steelworker, would rise to become engineer at the local factory.

15

Russian deserters, returning home from the front in World War I. Popular feeling against involvement in the war was so strong that it contributed substantially to the collapse of the tsarist government in 1917.

Discipline at the school was very strict, and the curriculum was rigorous. In addition to biology, chemistry, physics, world history, and mathematics, compulsory courses included the study of Latin, French, and German. Brezhnev was ambitious and worked hard, but remained only a mediocre student. A former classmate who later settled in the United States recalled that Brezhnev rarely spoke up in class, had difficulty with foreign languages, and only did well in Russian.

Although the school was not run by the clergy, a strong religious influence was present there. Each day began with prayers. A familiar figure to the students was Father Konstantin, the local Russian Orthodox priest. On special occasions, such as national holidays, he held services for the students in the school auditorium.

When they first entered the school the boys were given a set of rules about appropriate behavior, and these rules were strictly enforced. Uniforms had to be clean and tidy; a missing button was cause enough for punishment. When a teacher entered the classroom, students rose from their seats and sat down only when permission was given to do so. Outside school, the boys were required to take off their caps and bow if they passed by a teacher.

Brezhnev entered the klassicheskaya gimnaziya when he was not yet nine years old. By the time he graduated six years later — in 1921 — his world would turn upside down. Brezhnev, in the years between childhood and adolescence, was to experience firsthand the disasters of World War I, the Russian Revolution of 1917, and the subsequent civil war. From these early brushes with death, Brezhnev learned lessons in survival and adaptability that he would use for the rest of his life.

War made its first imprint on Kamenskoye through the requisitioning of horses. Soon all men of eligible age were conscripted into the army with the exception of most of the steelworkers. It was necessary to keep the plant operating for the war effort; Brezhnev's father thus escaped military duty at the front.

It was not long before the more serious effects of war made themselves felt in the town. Food became scarce. Increasing numbers of deserters and refugees swelled the population and soon aggravated the hunger problem.

But the increased number of mouths to feed, combined with the scarcity of food, was not the only serious problem. Russia's entry into the war was very unpopular with the Russian people. As news of the massive casualties and desertions trickled back from the front, political unrest and revolutionary agitation against the tsarist government increased. The Brezhnev family, however, had always been largely apolitical and had taken little interest in agitation, protests, and strikes. By and large they remained so throughout the six years of war, revolution, and civil strife.

In March 1917 the 300-year-old Romanov dynasty was toppled. The Provisional Government, headed by Alexander Kerensky, assumed control. This news was greeted with some relief in Kamenskoye, as well as the rest of the country. Finally, it was hoped, Russia would pull out of the war. Kerensky's government, however, made a fatal mistake. It pledged to continue the unpopular war, and the result was more domestic discontent and upheaval.

Economic life came to a standstill almost overnight and famine, deprivation, death, and disease reigned supreme.
—JOHN DORNBERG
Brezhnev biographer, on the effect of the civil war on the Ukraine

In November 1917 Vladimir Ilich Lenin, leader of the Communist Bolshevik party, staged another revolution in Petrograd and seized power from the weak Provisional Government. Lenin pledged an end to the war, no matter the cost, and thereby won more popular support for the Bolsheviks.

But Lenin had more items on his revolutionary agenda than simply withdrawing from the war. His goals encompassed massive social and political change. Not only were political associations of religious, monarchist, or right-wing leanings prohibited, but so were other leftist revolutionary parties. These included the Mensheviks, Social Revolutionaries, and anarchists.

Although the Bolsheviks were strong enough to seize power in Petrograd, they were not yet strong enough to extend it throughout the country. Lenin's October Revolution caused a civil war. (The Bolshevik uprising is commonly called the October Revolution because of the old-style calendar used in Russia at that time. The Soviets adopted the Western calendar only in 1918.) The White Army was formed by tsarist officers to fight the Bolsheviks (the Reds) and restore the tsar. During the confusion caused by the revolution, different nationalist movements throughout the old Russian Empire agitated for their independence. Consequently, in the first

A leftist revolutionary distributes newspapers in Moscow in 1917. The Bolsheviks were quick to recognize and use the power of propaganda in their campaign to educate and mobilize the Russian workers.

few months after the October Revolution, the Ukraine, Latvia, Lithuania, and Estonia all declared themselves independent states.

The three nations on Russia's Baltic Sea coast — Lithuania, Latvia, and Estonia — managed to keep their independence. The revolution provided them with an unexpected — and very welcome — opportunity to break away from Russian domination. The Ukraine, however, was a crucial area. The breadbasket of Russia, the Ukraine was necessary for national survival, and Lenin was not prepared to give it up. Although the Bolsheviks initially recognized the independent Republic of the Ukraine in November 1917, less than two months later the Red Army occupied the region.

Thus, the Ukraine experienced probably the most vicious fighting of the civil war. There were several different groups vying for control of the region. In addition to the Russians who were fighting each other — both the Red and White Armies — various independent native Ukrainian forces throughout the countryside were operating without any central control. These were largely guerrilla bands with loyalties to diverse groups: some were anarchist, others nationalist, and yet others simply disorganized groups of peasants. At times some of these bands joined forces with the White Army to fight the Reds;

General Lavr Kornilov (third from left), commander in chief of the White Army, 1917. During the civil war, the southern Ukraine was alternately occupied by the Red and White Armies. Brezhnev witnessed the devastation wrought by both sides.

19

First detachment of Red Guards from the Treugolnik Mills in Petrograd. The Bolsheviks organized such groups in a display of force to suppress imperialist sympathies. As an ethnic Russian and urban worker, Brezhnev supported the new Communist regime.

less often they joined the Red Army to fight the Whites. Mostly, however, they fought both.

As was the case with many other Ukrainian towns, the control of Kamenskoye changed hands several times between 1918 and 1921. When the Red Army occupied the town in early 1918, executions of all threatening or potentially threatening people began, including priests, intellectuals, members of the middle class, and Ukrainian nationalists. Bodies were dumped in the town square. When the Whites overcame the Reds, scores of revolutionaries were executed. The first effects of the October Revolution in Kamenskoye had resulted in the flight of almost all the foreign managers of the steel factory. The factory, already hampered in production because of the war with Germany, shut down entirely and remained closed until 1925.

For three more years, each time control of Kamenskoye changed hands, there were more killings. The inhabitants of the town did not themselves always remain innocent bystanders to the terror. Even some of Brezhnev's classmates, often no older than 12 or 13, participated in the civil war. One of them, the son of a barber, joined the White Army. When it occupied Kamenskoye, he arrested his former Russian literature teacher and shot him. The director of the girls' school, together with his family, met a similar fate; one of his former students became an executioner for the *Cheka* (the dreaded Bolshevik secret police) and shot the entire family in the town square.

Yet young Leonid Brezhnev did not participate in any of these activities. It may be that his sympathies lay more with the Bolsheviks, as was common for most of the industrial workers in the town, but his feelings were never translated into actions. In 1921 he graduated from high school, together with what remained of his original class: in 1915 more than 40 boys had started school with Brezhnev; by 1921, only 15 remained.

Soon after graduating from high school, Brezhnev joined a vocational program in metallurgy (the extraction and uses of metals) organized by an unemployed steel worker in Kamenskoye, and he stayed in the program until 1923. He then left Kamenskoye and enrolled in a four-year agricultural program at the Technicum for Land Utilization and Reclamation in nearby Kursk. This opportunity was made possible because Brezhnev finally made a political move. In 1923, six years after the Bolshevik revolution, he joined the *Komsomol*, the Young Communist League.

Brezhnev's decision to join the Komsomol, however, was based not on ideological reasons as much as pragmatic ones. He was ambitious; he wished to upgrade his position in life. The Bolsheviks — who by now had evolved into the Communist party of the Soviet Union (CPSU) — had won their struggle for power, and the new Soviet government wanted to recruit young cadres, such as Brezhnev, for its party organizations and, consequently, the best jobs in the country. Brezhnev had the right credentials — he was from a working-class family and was Russian in origin. Whether he really understood the theories of Marxism-Leninism — the Communist ideology of the CPSU — did not matter at this stage. The Communist party would take care of that through intensive teaching and indoctrination beginning in the Komsomol. What mattered was that he be loyal to the party. Brezhnev even then understood this very well, and he set about with determination to prove his trustworthiness to the party.

The golden age is coming; people will live without laws or punishment, doing of their own free will what is good, and just.
—Bolshevik slogan

2

The Making of a Party Cadre

Russia in the 1920s was not an easy place in which to live. It was a country devastated by long years of revolution, war, terror, and hunger. The victorious Communist revolutionaries still felt insecure and held on tightly to their newly acquired power. Their survival, they believed, depended on eliminating all threats, real or imaginary. At the same time, they saw themselves as endowed with a higher calling — the creation of the world's first revolutionary Communist society. Not only did they have to bring this society into existence, but they also needed to make it work.

The new society was to have none of the corrupt and fundamentally unfair features of the old one. There would be no more aristocracy, no privileged bourgeoisie, or middle class that took the profits from and reaped the benefits of the workers' labor. The country would be organized into a workers' state, where everyone would share equally in the nation's wealth.

Religion — particularly Russian Orthodoxy, long the ally of the tsarist monarchy — was seen by the

A soldier guards a factory in the 1920s. In the early years of the Bolshevik regime, the state took control of all industry, trade, and agriculture to restore some order and economic stability to the country.

SOVFOTO

Hierarchs of the Russian Orthodox church. The Orthodox church did not fare well under the Bolsheviks. Its association with the Romanov dynasty and the traditional authority of the clergy was intolerable to the Leninist government.

party to be the spiritual oppressor of the masses and was to be abolished. Atheism, according to the party, was the hallmark of a progressive society.

All private enterprise was to be abolished. The state, in the name of the working class, would take over foreign and domestic trade. Industry and agriculture were to be nationalized. There was no need for any political parties, because the ruling Communists believed they fully represented the people of the Soviet Union.

The Soviet challenge was to make reality fit the revolutionary agenda, and the new leaders wasted no time in setting about their task. Lenin, however, foresaw that before a new structure of society could be erected or heavy industry developed or rapid modernization implemented, people had to be fed.

Food, in the early 1920s, came predominantly from the Russian peasant, who tilled his own private plot. The Communists, whose power base came from the urban workers, distrusted the peasants. The peasants were bound to the traditions of their villages — traditions that had remained unchanged for centuries. Mostly illiterate, they lived in a world where the unquestioned authorities had been the tsar and the church.

The peasants, traditionally opposed to change, had little reason to shift their allegiance automatically to the new leaders. They knew nothing of Marxist theory and remained unimpressed by the high-minded slogans coming from the Communists. They knew only of crops and the changing seasons and were concerned with improving their daily lives.

Lenin realized that the prosperity of the peasant had a direct relationship to the prosperity of the country. In the mid-1920s only 18 percent of the Soviet Union's population lived in towns and cities; the rest were in the countryside. Thus, if the peasant was well fed, if conditions were favorable for him to grow more food, then the Soviet Union would not starve, and the Communist party could continue consolidating its power.

Lenin therefore introduced the New Economic Policy (commonly known as NEP). NEP was ideological heresy, for it allowed a degree of private enter-

The recovery of the Soviet Union after World War I and the revolution depended largely on the peasants, especially in the Ukraine, who were responsible for producing grain to feed the population. Brezhnev completed four years of training at Kursk Land Technicum to teach peasants how to use the land more productively.

SOVFOTO

prise, which Marxist theory held as the root of capitalist evil. There was a great deal of dissension in the party about NEP, but not enough to cause anyone to challenge Lenin's authority in implementing the policy.

NEP was a compromise; its purpose was to give the Soviet economy, ravaged by years of warfare, an opportunity to recover. The Communists kept control of finance and heavy industry but allowed private enterprise in small businesses and among the peasant farmers. A basic goal of the program was to aid the Russian peasant in producing more food. Immediately after the revolution the new government, to ensure food supplies for the Red Army and the cities, imposed grain requisitioning on the peasants and prohibited them from selling whatever surplus they had. The result had been a famine, for the peasants simply refused to till the land. But under NEP, peasants no longer had to meet forced quotas. They paid a tax instead and could now sell their surplus crops. In addition, the party sent agricultural specialists into the countryside to help peasants better utilize the land, which was often inefficiently tilled.

Leonid Brezhnev, having just joined the Komsomol, arrived at the Kursk Land Technicum to acquire this agricultural training. The four-year higher educational institution specialized in teaching young people to survey and set boundaries on tracts of land, as well as to chart land holdings and consolidate them. Lenin's NEP was a great success — so great, in fact that the Communists became alarmed. Their "minor" concessions to private enterprise had resulted in the growth of a nascent middle class: the so-called nepmen (prosperous businessmen and retailers) and the *kulaks*, wealthy peasant farmers who were profiting from the sale of their produce. Something had to be done to prevent the further erosion of party control over the economy, but the CPSU had been caught up in more immediate political concerns.

By the time Brezhnev graduated from the Kursk Land Technicum in 1927, the political winds were blowing in a different direction. Lenin had died in

1924, and there was a fierce power struggle within the party to determine his successor. Joseph Stalin, an opponent of NEP from the beginning, was the ultimate victor.

Lenin had warned that giving power to Stalin would be a grave mistake, and Stalin eventually proved him right. He eliminated, often violently, all potential rivals among the party's top leadership and brought in new, fresh recruits who had no existing loyalties to one faction or another. These people often owed their rapid rise through the party ranks to the vacancies created by Stalin's murderous purges.

Brezhnev was one of these young recruits. Throughout the 1930s, his rise in the party was due as much to these purges as it was to the unswerving obedience he displayed in carrying out Stalin's mandate. Brezhnev may not have fully understood the ideological differences that existed among factions of the party, but he did understand who wielded power. He toed the Stalinist line.

Brezhnev's first assignment after graduating from the Kursk Land Technicum was in Belorussia, in the Kokhanovsky district, 300 miles west of Moscow. However, his job as a land surveyor and consolidator was secondary to the goal of implementing government policies in the countryside, regardless of how these policies affected the peasant. Indeed, the pervasive Communist distrust and contempt for the peasantry, which Lenin had succeeded in restraining during NEP, now broke through in full force. Stalin's first Five-Year Plan in 1928 announced the beginning of collectivization, the consolidation of all the agricultural land under the direction of the state. There were two kinds of holdings: state farms, called *sovkhozy*, or collective farms, known as *kolkhozy*.

On the sovkhozy peasants were hired labor, paid hourly wages, just like workers in the factories. The kolkhozy, on the other hand, were technically owned by the groups of peasants that worked them. These workers were also paid, but their wages were entirely dependent on how much money the farm made. In addition, peasants who worked on the

Throw your bourgeois humanitarianism on the garbage heap and act like Bolsheviks. Destroy the kulak agents wherever they raise their heads.
—M. M. KHATAYEVICH
party chief of
Dnepropetrovsk, to
party members

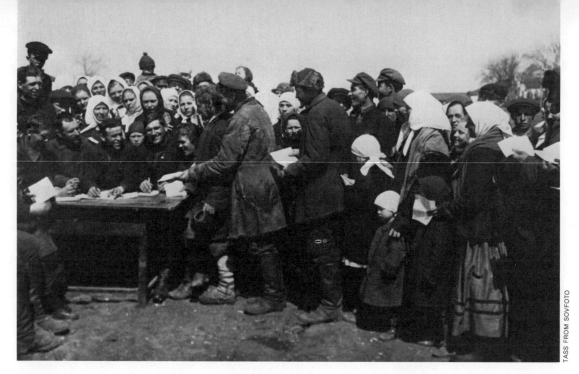

Peasants apply for acceptance to a collective farm. Stalin employed young party members, including Brezhnev, to convince the peasantry to join either state or collective farms.

kolkhozy were under obligation to sell a fixed amount of their produce to the state, at artificially low prices set by the government. The kolkhoz was the more common type of farm.

At first collectivization was to be voluntary, and a large part of Brezhnev's job was to convince the peasants of the new system's benefits — less physical hardship, new equipment, the rapid modernization of agricultural techniques.

But the skeptical peasants resisted joining the collective farms, and the government began resorting to force. A campaign was undertaken to set the poorer and middle class peasants against the kulaks. If the kulak did not willingly give up his grain to the government, it was taken from him. If he resisted enlisting in either a collective or state farm, he was forced to join. If he refused to give up his own land for collective farming, then he was deported forcibly to Siberia.

Millions of Russian peasants met just such a fate. It is estimated that by the time the collectivization program had been completed in the late 1930s, more than 7 million peasants had been uprooted from their homes, most of whom were relocated to Siberia.

Brezhnev's second assignment was in the Ural

Mountains, in the Bisertsky district, 1,000 miles east of Moscow. By the time he arrived there in 1929, a number of important events had occurred in his life. He was now married — to a nurse named Viktoriya Petrovna — and was also a father. A daughter, Galina, was born in Bisertsky that same year. More important was Brezhnev's admission to the Communist party as a candidate, or nonvoting member. He became a full member with voting privileges in 1931.

During the short time Brezhnev was in the Urals, he rose quickly through the ranks. Within a year of his arrival, he had replaced his boss at the Bisertsky Land Department. He was largely responsible for the repressive measures undertaken in the district to force peasants to give up their land and join the collective farms. By 1930, 30 percent of Brezhnev's district was collectivized, and he was promoted to deputy chairman of the Land Management Board for the entire Urals region. Shortly thereafter, he was sent to the capital to study at the prestigious Moscow Agricultural Academy. Brezhnev's unquestioning loyalty and devotion to Stalin's collectivization policy brought him to the attention of his superiors.

Yet, he did not stay long at the Agricultural Academy. In fact, he left agriculture altogether and returned home to Kamenskoye, where he joined his father and brother at the local steel factory. He moved into a two-room apartment with Viktoriya and Galina.

The abrupt change in Brezhnev's career has never been fully explained. Why would a young man who already had some experience as an administrator and official go back to the life of a simple worker? There is speculation that he got into trouble in Moscow, either personal, academic, or political, and was expelled or left on his own. It is unlikely that Brezhnev committed a political blunder. In those terror-filled days, when Stalin was tightening his grip on the country, anyone who had a political blemish on his record did not get very far. Such an individual was soon purged from the party and either deported to Siberia or executed without explanation.

Brezhnev (third from left) at a session of the party branch of the Metallurgical College in Dneprodzerzhinsk. From 1931 to 1935 Brezhnev studied at the college, thus changing the focus of his career from agriculture to industry.

Back in Kamenskoye, however, Brezhnev thrived. During the next four years, his life was a whirlwind of activity. At the factory, he had a variety of different jobs — starting out as a boiler stoker, then becoming a machine oiler, fitter, and finally, a gas purification machine operator. He also enrolled at at the newly opened M. I. Arsenichev Metallurgical Institute to study engineering at night. He became more active politically and was appointed party secretary at the institute. In 1933 he became director of the institute's Workers' Faculty, a type of technical vocational program set up to train people who lacked the necessary qualifications to attend a technical institute. That same year, there was another addition to his young family—a son, Yuri, was born.

Although Brezhnev had turned his sights from a career in agriculture to one in industry, he still participated in the collectivization campaign. Through his position as party secretary at the Metallurgical Institute, Brezhnev organized Komsomol student brigades to go into the surrounding countryside and take part in the forced requisitioning of food from the peasants.

The student brigades, like the other official requisitioners, were empowered with the right to take any and all food from the peasants in order to break resistance to collectivization. They tore apart whole villages. They ripped open floorboards and walls and destroyed farm buildings and living quarters, taking whatever was edible. The peasants grew increasingly desperate and would sneak out at night to cut a few grains of wheat from their own fields. They were then arrested for stealing the "state's" grain. The peasants began eating twigs and leaves. Reports of cannibalism circulated. According to Brezhnev biographer Paul J. Murphy, criminals murdered small children, whom they then quartered and offered as salted meat.

More dead than alive, peasants with bloated bellies streamed from the countryside into the towns seeking relief, even though they were prohibited from leaving their native villages without special permission. Trucks rumbled nightly along the roads, collecting corpses. Meanwhile, the requisitioners — the grain collectors, Komsomol brigades, party activists, and special police units — were all well fed. They had access to special stores of food, and were unaffected by the famine that destroyed the peasantry. Indeed, while the rural populace starved city dwellers had food, and the Soviet Union even *exported* grain.

As a result of the brutal collectivization of the early 1930s, it is estimated that nearly 7 million people, perhaps 5 million of whom were Ukrainians, starved

They hurled themselves on the region like a pack of locusts and seized everything edible.
—MALCOLM MUGGERIDGE
correspondent for the *Manchester Guardian*, on the activities of the army and the secret police

SOVFOTO

Maxim Gorky (right) was one of the few writers to survive under Stalin (left), who instituted a policy of strict censorship. Stalin regularly used the writings of well-known figures as propaganda to paint a rosy picture of the benefits of his policies.

to death. The famine, artificially created by the Soviet government, succeeded in breaking the firm resistance of the kulaks to Soviet control throughout the Ukraine.

On the heels of the collectivization campaign, Stalin initiated a wholesale purge of the party itself. In this way, he removed the last of the old Bolshevik revolutionaries, including such renowned figures as Lev Kamenev, Grigori Zinoviev, and Nikolai Bukharin, each of whom had been proposed by Lenin as possible successors. After 1934 Stalin's purges took on an unparalleled dimension. The assassination of Sergei Kirov, the Leningrad party chief, on December 1, 1934, gave the dictator the excuse he needed to unleash the secret police — at this time known as the NKVD (People's Commissariat of Internal Affairs) — to rout out "fascist agents," "traitors," and "anti-Soviet saboteurs" from the party. Stalin also purged the military, because he believed it was capable of overthrowing him. The most brilliant military men were executed. Thus, terror in the 1930s was by no means confined to the countryside.

It is estimated that between 1 and 10 million people died as a result of Stalin's purges. Those who were lucky enough to escape death often found themselves in the *gulags*, or concentration camps, together with their former accusers and interrogators. No one was immune from the dreaded midnight visit by the secret police.

Brezhnev, however, not only survived during these years — he prospered. After graduating from the Metallurgical Institute as an engineer in 1935, he was drafted into the territorial army for one year. He served at a tank tactics school in the Transbaikal region in Siberia and became his platoon's sergeant, then its political officer, whose duty it was to reinforce party ideology among the soldiers. In 1936 he returned to Kamenskoye, which had been renamed Dneprodzerzhinsk after the first director of the secret police, Feliks Dzerzhinsky. For a year Brezhnev was the director of the local technical college. In May 1937 he was elected deputy town mayor in Dneprodzerzhinsk. (The party chose the candidates for

NOVOSTI FROM SOVFOTO

Feliks Dzerzhinsky, first director of the NKVD, the Soviet secret police. On evidence submitted by the police, Stalin began a series of purges to rid the Soviet Union of his real and imagined enemies. Brezhnev was not seen as a threat by Stalin and so survived the purges.

all elections; the voters merely "elected" whomever was on the ballot.) It was Brezhnev's first full-time government post.

To a great degree Brezhnev owed his success to being in the right place at the right time and to belonging to a younger generation not yet perceived as a threat by Stalin. Almost always, Brezhnev was promoted to fill positions left vacant by those who fell victim to Stalin's tyranny. Even if Brezhnev had wanted to oppose Stalin, he could not. The price easily could have been his own life and very possibly the lives of his family as well. But Brezhnev does not seem to have exhibited any major doubts about his role in carrying out Stalin's policies during that period. He believed that the excesses were justified by the goal. In this, he was typical of many young Communist functionaries, called *apparatchiks*, of his time. They were convinced that only extreme vigilance could protect the party from traitors. Brezhnev believed that in order to build a socialist society, any methods — seemingly even criminal and inhumane ones — were justifiable. And a loyal apparatchik did not question Stalin.

3

Patron and Protégé

In 1938 Brezhnev's political career became inextricably linked with that of another staunch Stalinist — Nikita Sergeevich Khrushchev, who in January of that year was made first secretary of the Ukrainian Communist party.

The previous year Stalin had sent Khrushchev to purge the Ukrainian party, believing that it exhibited too strong a tendency toward Ukrainian nationalism and showed insufficient loyalty to him. Khrushchev proved quite adept at his job: by January 1938, when he was appointed to the top party post in the Ukraine, the Ukrainian party was decimated. Most of the provincial government officials, even at the lower district and regional levels, were arrested and executed or simply disappeared.

In order to stay in favor himself, Khrushchev quickly needed to restructure the Ukrainian party and government along strict Stalinist lines. He began to search for trustworthy apparatchiks to fill all the vacant posts. Brezhnev qualified as an ideal candidate. He was a loyal Stalinist: his record since

Like Khrushchev, from whom he learned the political ropes, [Brezhnev] is a master of the art of patronage and influence peddling.
—JOHN DORNBERG
Brezhnev biographer

Brezhnev (center) in the Victory Day Parade in Red Square, June 24, 1945. By the close of World War II, Brezhnev had succeeded in advancing himself in the military and the party. As a political commissar he was deeply involved in aiding the Soviet takeover of formerly independent territories.

SOVFOTO

Khrushchev with Stalin, 1932. As first secretary of the Ukrainian Communist party in 1938, Khrushchev appointed Brezhnev to offices left vacant when Stalin purged the Ukrainian party. From that time on, Brezhnev's future was linked with Khrushchev's.

graduating from the Kursk Land Technicum 10 years earlier proved it. He was a Russian who was familiar with the Ukraine — a combination Stalin favored, given his intense distrust of ethnic Ukrainians. He had a technical background, always useful to the party in its drive for industrial modernization. Moreover, there was no political skeleton in Brezhnev's closet.

Brezhnev first came to Khrushchev's attention through one of the new Ukrainian party chief's aides, Demyan Korotchenko. Korotchenko, along with a few other of Khrushchev's top men, was entrusted to find suitable party members, such as Brezhnev. In all, 1,600 party members were brought into the Ukrainian governing apparatus in 1938, and 300 of these became directors of various departments. Brezhnev was one of the new directors; his new appointment was head of the Department of Ideology and Indoctrination at the Dnepropetrovsk regional level.

Brezhnev's political future now depended on Nikita Khrushchev. Khrushchev's role was to protect and promote those protégés who were useful to him, in order to further his own interests and expand his own influence. In turn, Brezhnev, as one of Khrushchev's men, would support and implement his patron's policies in the Ukraine, making Khrushchev look successful to his patron, Stalin. It was a well-ordered system; the rules were unwritten, but everyone understood them.

On the lower levels, Brezhnev started to build up his own power base. In 1938 the "Dnieper Mafia," as Brezhnev's entourage of supporters came to be called, first began to take shape. Many of Brezhnev's associates and subordinates from this time would be found in the highest government and party posts 30 years later.

In May 1938 Brezhnev was transferred to the regional capital of Dnepropetrovsk, 22 miles from his hometown, to begin his new job. A year later, when the position was created, he became the Dnepropetrovsk region's secretary for propaganda.

As chief censor and propagandist, Brezhnev was responsible for making sure that the party's views — or more accurately, Stalin's views — on any issue were correctly explained and disseminated to the people of his region. All literature, conferences, discussion groups, and political seminars had to pass Brezhnev's inspection. Brezhnev made sure these reflected the correct party line. In addition, he stifled any information that reflected badly on Stalin and the party.

It was a very visible position, which entailed both risks and rewards. If his superiors thought he was doing a good job, he could claim the credit. But if not, there was no way to duck the responsibility. A misplaced phrase, a greeting to Stalin that was not effusive enough, too much or not enough emphasis on one of the party's directives — these were enough to damage Brezhnev. But Brezhnev, in his energetic, yet methodical way, faithfully and effectively did his job.

One of Brezhnev's first assignments was to promote an intense "Russification" campaign in his

> *The late thirties were a time for jubilation — artificial jubilation. We read jubilant books, listened to jubilant speeches, and saw jubilant movies.*
> —emigré from Dnepropetrovsk, commenting on Brezhnev's propaganda campaign

region. In fact, Stalin's massive assault on Ukrainian culture was being carried out throughout the Ukraine. Intent on destroying Ukrainian nationalism and separate identity, Stalin ordered that Ukrainian history be rewritten to place greater emphasis on the "benevolent" and "progressive" Russian influence. Prominent Ukrainians who were interested in preserving their national culture were branded "bourgeois nationalists," and there were attempts to link them with spying for Poland or Nazi Germany. Compulsory Russian language courses were introduced in schools, and Russian became the language in which all official business was conducted in the republic. Brezhnev's task was to promote all things Russian and denigrate everything Ukrainian.

Brezhnev's second major propaganda campaign consisted of denouncing the growing power of Adolf Hitler and the Nazis in Germany. Throughout the 1930s, Hitler's fascist regime was portrayed as the worst threat to the Soviet Union's territorial integrity and communist system. During the purges, standard accusations against those labeled enemies of the state included "fascist spies" and "Nazi saboteurs."

Suddenly, in August 1939, the Soviet Union signed a nonaggression treaty with Germany. In the Molotov-Ribbentrop Pact (titled after the names of the Soviet and German foreign ministers), Germany and the Soviet Union agreed to refrain from declaring war on one another. In addition, in a secret protocol of the pact, they carved up the territories of several eastern European countries. Western Poland would go to the Nazis, while eastern Poland and the Baltic states of Latvia, Lithuania, and Estonia would be taken by the Soviet Union. On September 1, 1939, Germany invaded Poland, and World War II began. Soon after, the Soviet Union occupied the Baltic states and Poland's eastern regions.

In an abrupt reversal, portrayals of the Nazis as vicious enemies disappeared from Soviet propaganda. Any reference to Germany took on a neutral tone. Brezhnev was responsible for making sure

that all information in his region reflected this new turn of events. For the first two years of the war, the two ideological enemies remained very unlikely allies.

However, Stalin, a year and a half after the war began, set out to rebuild the military he had crippled through the purges. In February 1941 Stalin ordered heavy industry to start producing more weapons, missiles, tanks, and other war materials. He then created regional-level posts of secretary for the defense industry. Brezhnev was appointed defense secretary for the Dnepropetrovsk region. He was responsible for turning as many of the region's industries as possible to the production of military hardware. All his policies were first approved by Khrushchev.

The Dnepropetrovsk region was one of the most important industrial centers in the Ukraine. Chemical, metallurgical, and transportation industries predominated. Brezhnev was able to convert two factories to producing small arms, as well as to step up the manufacture of gun barrels. The steel factory in his home town, Dneprodzerzhinsk, began limited production of ammunition and artillery shells. It is estimated that the production of armaments in the region increased about 60 percent.

A German prisoner of war sits beside a gun destroyed by Soviet artillery. The Soviets, forced to retreat by the brutally swift German advance in June 1941, attempted to dismantle or destroy anything the Germans could use. One of Brezhnev's first responsibilities was to take apart factories in the Ukraine and ship them to the interior.

TASS FROM SOVFOTO

Brezhnev (kneeling, far right) with the 18th Army, in which he served as a political commissar. During the war, political commissars were highly feared officers whose job was to maintain strict party control within the military.

But it was all too little, too late. Only four months elapsed between the time Stalin started to mobilize the country and Hitler invaded the Soviet Union on June 22, 1941. Chaos prevailed; the invasion had caught the Soviets by surprise. The German army, with its lightning-fast *blitzkrieg* strategy, quickly advanced into Soviet territory, reaching the Ukrainian capital, Kiev, in less than a month. Brezhnev's job now entailed dismantling those factories that were not producing armaments and shipping them into the Soviet interior, coordinating the remaining industrial resources to step up even greater weapons production, and laying waste to all that could not be shipped out so the approaching German army would not be able to use anything left behind.

By late August 1941 the Germans captured Dnepropetrovsk. Brezhnev's wife, two children, mother, and sister had stayed in the town almost until the end. They were evacuated on one of the last trains and traveled to safety in the Soviet central Asian republic of Kazakhstan, where they remained until the end of the war.

Brezhnev had joined the Red Army a month earlier. He was first assigned to the Southern Army Group as a lieutenant colonel. By April 1942 he was promoted to colonel and transferred to the 18th Army, where he remained for most of the war. Before the war ended he attained the rank of major general.

But Brezhnev was not a military man. Indeed, his political background in the party was essential to his wartime role. Brezhnev became a political commissar.

The role of political commissar was unique to the Red Army. His job was to ensure party control over the military, sometimes by persuasion, sometimes by force. The political commissar had to show that the party was in the forefront of the battle with the enemy — that fighting for the homeland was synonymous with fighting for the party. It was his job to instill patriotism, discipline, and optimism in the officers and enlisted men.

It was also the commissar's job to capture those soldiers who deserted the army. In the early months of the war, desertion was such a common occurrence that political commissars were given the right to punish the escapees on the spot, and executions were a daily affair. The commissars maintained close contact with the NKVD and with special party units positioned behind the front lines that spied on the soldiers to find the deserters, the politically suspect, or insufficiently patriotic recruits. Officially, the commissars were not authorized to plan or implement military strategy, although it was a foolish commander who would ignore the "suggestions" of his unit's political officer.

The political commissars were generally hated for their military incompetence and feared for their role as police watchdogs. Yet the presence of political officers did make a difference. Whether out of fear of being denounced to the NKVD or in response to the rousing patriotic speeches often made by the commissars, the soldiers responded with increased aggression and determination. In fact, the commis-

Soviet soldiers set up a USSR signpost on Soviet territory in 1944 upon its liberation from the Germans. As early as 1944, Stalin had plans to annex territories liberated by the Soviets from German occupation.

German soldiers captured by the Red Army in Czechoslovakia. In the areas liberated by the 18th Army — Transcarpathia and Czechoslovakia — Brezhnev's job was to promote ties with the Soviet Union. Using all his propaganda skills, Brezhnev was instrumental in bringing both areas under Soviet domination.

SOVFOTO

sars were considered so influential and dangerous that Hitler ordered them to be executed immediately when captured.

While Brezhnev was strict and ruthless when he had to be, there is also evidence that he genuinely concerned himself with the welfare of the men under his command. There are also reliable accounts that Brezhnev actually joined troops in the trenches, and that he had a few narrow escapes from death. During the war he was awarded the Order of the Red Banner for bravery, which lends some authenticity to his claims of exemplary leadership.

Brezhnev stayed with the 18th Army in battles on the Black Sea, at Novorossisk, Rostov-on-Don, and across the Ukraine. After the Battle of Stalingrad ended in a Soviet victory, the war turned against the Germans. The 18th Army moved steadily west, recapturing Dnepropetrovsk, Kiev, Berdichev, and Zhitomir. By autumn 1944 the Ukraine was once more in Soviet hands. As it pursued the retreating Germans, the Red Army went beyond the prewar Soviet border. Brezhnev and the 18th Army occupied territories previously under Czechoslovak rule.

As the 18th Army moved westward on its way into Czechoslovakia, it occupied a mountainous region called Transcarpathia.

Bordered by Romania to the south, Hungary and Czechoslovakia to the west, Poland to the north, and the Ukraine to the east, Transcarpathia had an ethnically mixed population of about 500,000 people. Because Transcarpathia previously had been part of Czechoslovakia, Stalin promised the London-based Czech government-in-exile in 1943 that the region would revert to Czechoslovakia after the war. But, as happened throughout Eastern Europe, once the Red Army arrived, an entirely different agenda was put into operation.

Brezhnev was pivotal to the operations in Transcarpathia and Czechoslovakia. While still retaining his duties as political commissar in the army, he was charged with bringing Transcarpathia into the Soviet Union. This was not just a simple matter of the region's military occupation; that had already been achieved. He was to turn the social, economic, and political situation in the area to Soviet advantage. Under the guise of legality, he had to make it appear that a broadly based, popularly supported cross section of the population desired to become part of the Soviet Ukrainian republic.

It was not an easy job, but Brezhnev, a master of propaganda, knew what was needed. By promising the populace free elections, he dispelled fears of an imminent Soviet takeover. He courted and reassured the Communist party's traditional enemies, such as religious leaders and non-Communist politicians, of the peaceful intent of the Soviet Union. Initially, no terror or repression was used on the people; he needed their assent and good will. Brezhnev appealed to Transcarpathia's Ukrainians by blanketing the region with posters and pamphlets exalting the good life to be had by uniting with the Ukraine. He exploited the differences in class and social status among the various nationalities in the region. He offered landless peasants the confiscated properties of formerly well-to-do landowners, knowing full well that with collectivization as the next stage, the peasants would not keep the land for long.

> *Now Soviet people appeared as liberators and it was very important not to discredit this humane mission in any way.*
> —LEONID BREZHNEV
> on the liberation
> of Czechoslovakia

SOVFOTO

Soviet soldiers celebrate the end of the war. The Soviets now faced the enormous task of rebuilding their shattered country.

Having lured representatives of various independent political views to join a coalition dominated by pro-Soviet Communists, Brezhnev then had these independents isolated and expelled, one by one. Where necessary, he used force and terror — those who could not be coerced into compliance were either murdered or deported. Thousands of people perished.

By the end of the war Brezhnev had moved on to Czechoslovakia, where he was again involved in setting up a pro-Soviet regime in the newly liberated country. The tactics used in Transcarpathia were repeated in Czechoslovakia. On June 24, 1945, a month after the war ended, Brezhnev marched in the Victory Parade in Moscow's Red Square. But he left Moscow the same evening, returning to Transcarpathia to add the finishing touches in molding it into a truly Soviet region. The Czechoslovak president, Edvard Beneš, had been pressured by Stalin into ceding the area to the Soviet Union.

Brezhnev left Transcarpathia in August 1946 to be reunited with his family, whom he had not seen for five years. They had already returned to Dnepropetrovsk. Daughter Galina was now a 17-year-old. Yuri, who had recently joined the Pioneers, the party organization for youngsters, was 13.

Upon his return to the Ukraine, Brezhnev was appointed first party secretary of the industrially important Zaporozhye region. Zaporozhye was as devastated as the rest of the country. The people of the Soviet Union had suffered terribly in the war. The nation had lost 20 million people; cities were little more than rubble heaps; fields were scorched and useless. The Ukraine, scene of much of the fighting, was particularly hard hit, for the Nazis, in their retreat, had destroyed as much as they could. The capital of the Zaporozhye region (also called Zaporozhye) lay in ruins; the local economy was at a virtual standstill.

Brezhnev's task was to rebuild the Zaporozhye Iron and Steel Works, known as Zaporozhstal, and the Dneproges, the enormous dam on the Dnieper River. Dneproges, the first large hydroelectric complex built in the Soviet Union, was of vital importance, providing much-needed energy for the region. Dneproges was relatively new; it had been completed with assistance from American technical specialists in the early 1930s. But it was severely damaged in the war. Zaporozhstal was in worse shape; engineers reported that the plant was more than two-thirds destroyed. Stalin wanted Dneproges repaired and Zaporozhstal to be producing sheet metal even before the 1946 Five-Year Plan deadline was up.

Brezhnev wasted no time. Working all day and night, he oversaw the rebuilding of the dam and the plant. He organized disparate groups of workers and set an overall schedule for the completion of the projects. He checked up, sometimes on an hourly basis, to see that the targets he had set were being met. He did not tolerate any delay and refused to consider the demands made on the workers by the superhuman pace. His career was at stake; he could not afford to fail.

While Brezhnev was rebuilding industry in the Dnieper Valley, in March 1947 his patron inexplicably fell from favor. Within one month Khrushchev was relieved of his positions as first secretary of the Communist party in the Ukraine, the Kiev regional committee, and the Kiev city committee. Khrushchev's fall meant that it was not long before a purge of his protégés would begin.

Brezhnev realized the precarious position he was in when Stalin himself contacted him to move the production schedule up for Zaporozhstal. Brezhnev redoubled his efforts to make the deadline. He now worked and slept on site, rarely going home. He instituted round-the-clock shifts. Workers were diverted from other important construction projects in the region. Slave labor — prisoners under the guard of the secret police — also provided added manpower. At the peak, there were 47,000 people working at Zaporozhstal.

Brezhnev regularly reported the progress of the reconstruction work. In six months Dneproges was operating. Brezhnev assured Stalin that Zaporozhstal would start production on schedule, and he kept his promise. The first furnace went into opera-

> *Like his wartime role, Brezhnev's performance in Zaporozhye appears to improve with every year that the accomplishments themselves recede into history.*
> —JOHN DORNBERG
> Brezhnev biographer

tion on June 30, 1947, and the first sheet metal produced by the plant was delivered the following October. In December 20,000 workers from Zaporozhstal were awarded the Order of Lenin. Brezhnev personally was presented his award by Stalin.

The fortunes of Brezhnev's patron also improved. By the end of 1947, in one of the reversals typical of Stalin, Khrushchev was back in favor, restored to his former position. Brezhnev left Zaporozhye to return to Dnepropetrovsk as first secretary of the regional party.

As party chief of his home region, Brezhnev was responsible for the overall state of affairs. He continued to put in a respectable performance rebuilding industry in the region. Brezhnev even made considerable progress in revitalizing agriculture, despite the fact that Soviet agriculture had not yet fully recovered from the effects of the war. Dnepropetrovsk was, in fact, the first Ukrainian region to

TASS FROM SOVFOTO

46

complete the quotas set for the 1948 harvest.

In 1950 Brezhnev left Dnepropetrovsk to become one of Khrushchev's top deputies in Moscow. Khrushchev himself had been brought to the capital to sort out the problems in national agriculture. After a number of months in Moscow, Brezhnev received a significant promotion. As in nearly all his promotions, Brezhnev stepped into the shoes of a purged official. He became the party chief of one of the Soviet Union's 15 republics, Moldavia.

Although territorially quite small, only slightly larger than the Dnepropetrovsk region, Moldavia was one of the most difficult areas of the Soviet Union to govern. The primary reason was that, like Transcarpathia, it had been forcibly annexed to the USSR only five years previously. Bordered on the west by Romania — of which it had been a part until the eve of World War II — and on all other sides by the Ukraine, Moldavia staunchly resisted Soviet occupation and domination. As a result, in the five years after the war, half a million people had been executed, imprisoned, or deported to Siberia.

When Brezhnev arrived in the republic's capital, Kishinev, he set out to crush Moldavian resistance. He began by enforcing collectivization policies in the republic. He attacked the leadership of the existing collective farms for not meeting their quotas. He instituted severe penalties for economic crimes against the kolkhozy. The new regional leader had resisting kulaks deported or shot, and to enforce his policies he brought his own strong-arm teams in from the Ukraine.

Brezhnev also set up a Russification program for Moldavia. In a campaign designed to disassociate Moldavians from their native culture and heritage, their Moldavian language, a dialect of Romanian, was "Russified." Moldavians now had to use the Cyrillic (Russian) alphabet; their use of the Latin alphabet was prohibited. Moldavian music, history, and literature came under severe scrutiny and harsh criticism. Immigration of Russians to Moldavia was promoted.

Brezhnev also built up and centralized the republic's propaganda machine. Thirty-five new news-

SOVFOTO

Moldavian women take a break from their work. Moldavia, like Transcarpathia, was taken over by the Soviets after the war. In his post as party chief of Moldavia, Brezhnev was once again required to oversee the assimilation, reorganization, collectivization, and Russification of the annexed territory.

papers were established to extol the virtues of Soviet society. All the press and information sources depicted the benefits that the Soviet way of life was bringing to Moldavia and never failed to underscore that Stalin's genius made it all possible. It was in Moldavia that Brezhnev met Konstantin Ustinovich Chernenko, head of the department of propaganda and agitation of the Moldavian Central Committee since 1948. Chernenko aided Brezhnev in the propaganda campaign to Russify the Moldavians, and he subsequently became one of Brezhnev's early protégés.

In the autumn of 1952 Brezhnev's career took a sudden upswing when he catapulted to the top echelons of the ruling elite of the country. At the 19th Party Congress in October 1952, he was elected to the Central Committee, a body of about 125 members that represents the cream of the party's elite in the Soviet Union. The Central Committee then elected him a candidate, or nonvoting member of the expanded Presidium, the ruling body of the Soviet Communist party.

In late 1952 just as Brezhnev, having reached a national position, began to feel secure, rumors of another major purge arose. Soon the accusing finger would be pointed at all levels of the party bureaucracy, and the terror of the 1930s would once again reappear. But the purge never came. Stalin died in March 1953 before he could initiate it.

Children in the Jewish Children's Home in Vilnius, Lithuania. Religion posed a threat to the Soviet plan for a united, homogeneous state. Part of the assimilation program conducted by Brezhnev was aimed at subverting religion, which was condemned for dividing the loyalties of the people, whose only concern should be the state.

Khrushchev addresses a party meeting in 1955. Following Stalin's death in 1953, powerful party members, including Khrushchev, fought to succeed him. Brezhnev's future depended entirely upon Khrushchev's success in this political struggle.

The reaction to Stalin's death was curious. While political prisoners in the labor camps cheered, most people were simply stunned. For almost 25 years, Stalin had ruled with an iron fist. He controlled nearly every aspect of life; the people had been told repeatedly that only by Stalin's great leadership were they able to prosper. He had led them through the "Great Patriotic War," as the Soviets termed World War II. Life without Stalin was inconceivable to many.

The older generation in the party prepared for the inevitable power struggle. The first move was to demote those younger men who had come in with the 19th Party Congress. Thus, as quickly as he had been promoted only half a year earlier, Brezhnev was now stripped of his post in the Presidium and his membership on the Central Committee. Brezhnev's fate now depended even more on Khrushchev, who emerged in a position of considerable power after Stalin's death. As his patron locked horns with the other party bosses, Brezhnev sat by the sidelines quietly biding his time. Events, for the moment, were beyond his control.

It is not heroes that make history, but history that makes heroes.
—JOSEPH STALIN

49

4

De-Stalinization and the Thaw

The first months after Stalin's death were extremely turbulent for the party. Although a number of powerful men sat on the Presidium, including the staunch Stalinists Vyacheslav Molotov and Lazar Kaganovich and party ideologue and theoretician Mikhail Suslov, the contenders for Stalin's position came down to three individuals. These were Georgi Malenkov, whose power base was the Leningrad party machine, Lavrenti Beria, who, as head of the secret police since 1938, had the vast resources of this dreaded institution at his disposal, and Nikita Khrushchev.

Immediately after Stalin's death, Malenkov and Khrushchev concluded that it was necessary to oust Beria, who was using the secret police apparatus to secure power for himself. Beria was arrested in June 1953 and shot almost immediately thereafter. With Beria out of the way, Malenkov and Khrushchev turned on one another. Their battle would last four years, until Malenkov was finally defeated.

In 1953, however, both men shared more similarities than differences in what they thought the

Only let there be grain and the songs will come of themselves.
—LEONID BREZHNEV

Brezhnev and Premier Ibrahim Abboud of the Sudan cruise the Nile in 1961. In the early 1960s, Soviet foreign policy concentrated on relations with countries of Asia and Africa. As chief of state, Brezhnev traveled to these countries to court their leaders and convince them of the value of alliance with the Soviet Union.

SOVFOTO

Lavrenti Beria, Georgi Malenkov, and Anastas Mikoyan salute marchers in Red Square in 1949. Khrushchev and Malenkov joined forces to eliminate Beria, the head of the secret police, from the power struggle that followed Stalin's death. Later, Khrushchev emerged victorious over Malenkov.

Soviet Union's priorities should be. Unlike Molotov and Kaganovich, who favored continuing Stalinist policies, the two adversaries saw the need for a drastic change. Both thought that Soviet agriculture had been woefully neglected in the postwar drive to rebuild heavy industry. Both believed that the consumer sector of the economy needed to be developed to improve the general standard of living.

Where they differed — at least publicly — was in how to go about effecting the needed changes. Malenkov thought that the only way light industry could be developed was at the expense of the Soviet military-industrial complex. This, of course, alienated that entire sector from his camp. Khrushchev turned out to be the more astute politician. He saw no reason why one had to give up one for the other. The conflict split the top leadership, and by the end of 1953, the territory of each man was clearly established — Khrushchev became head of the party, while Malenkov controlled the government.

In the Soviet Union the party and the government are separate but parallel structures. All government officials are members of the party, but not all party officials necessarily hold a government post. A government minister one year can be appointed to a party position the next. Ultimately, the party wields the power; the government exists to carry out party directives. So Khrushchev felt he had the edge over Malenkov.

In an effort to eclipse Malenkov in grand style, in 1954 Khrushchev put forward a radical program to solve the country's agricultural problems, which were indeed serious. There were recurring grain shortages, less livestock than in the 1920s, and overall, a grossly inefficient system. Centralized planning, collectivization, and the war all contributed to the agricultural difficulties. To help solve the problems Malenkov wanted to provide more incentives to the peasants working on the existing kolkhozy. Khrushchev, however, proposed the cultivation of an entirely new part of the Soviet Union; in other words, he sought to provide the USSR with a second breadbasket.

When the agricultural experts heard the proposed area — Kazakhstan — and the scope of the project — to bring more than 50,000 square miles under the plow — they were convinced of its madness. But the sheer grandeur of the scheme appealed to some, and others agreed in principle with its aim. In any event, Khrushchev's plan, despite Malenkov's strong opposition, was adopted. The project became known as the "Virgin Lands Program." In the early months of 1954, Khrushchev assigned Brezhnev the task of making it a success.

Brezhnev, who had been assigned to a minor post in the navy administration after being stripped of his Presidium and Central Committee titles, was not appointed head of the project. Malenkov insisted on one of his own men for that position — Panteleimon Ponomarenko. The latter was appointed first secretary of the Kazakh regional party. Brezhnev was second secretary.

Brezhnev smarted under these conditions. He believed that Ponomarenko really intended not to help the Virgin Lands Program, but to sabotage it, for that would benefit his own patron, Malenkov. Never-

> *There was a yawning gap of confusion, disorganization, apathy, and corruption between promise and reality.*
> —JOHN DORNBERG
> Brezhnev biographer, on
> the Virgin Lands Program

theless, both men arrived as a team in the Kazakh capital, Alma Ata, in early February 1954.

Kazakhstan, primarily a prairie steppe region, located thousands of miles east of Moscow, is bordered by Uzbekistan to the southwest, China to the east, Siberia and the Ural Mountains to the north, and the Caspian Sea to the west. It is sparsely populated and is roughly equivalent in size to France. The weather in the area is notoriously unpredictable; farmers in the region often suffer from late frosts or severe droughts.

Brezhnev and Ponomarenko had to start from scratch. There were no towns, no villages, and very few people to cultivate the prairie steppe. As Brezhnev later recalled, "The development of the virgin lands was not just a matter of ploughing. It meant the building of housing, schools, hospitals, kindergartens, crèches, recreation centers and new roads, bridges, airfields and animal farms, grain elevators, storehouses, factories. In short, everything that people need to live a normal life and for modern farming."

Brezhnev greets workers in Kazakhstan, site of Khrushchev's Virgin Lands agricultural development program. Brezhnev provided crucial support for the Virgin Lands policy.

TASS FROM SOVFOTO

Brezhnev had only 20 months to make the project work. The first harvest, only half a year away, already had to show some results. Khrushchev's career, and therefore Brezhnev's, was riding on it. The call went out across the Soviet Union for volunteers to work the Virgin Lands. Thousands of young men and women responded. The conditions they found upon arrival were abysmal. There were no houses, only tents or rough huts, no running water, and no electricity. Meals were cooked on outside stoves or campfires. Transportation facilities were primitive; roads were unpaved, and the only suitable winter vehicles were sleighs. The agricultural equipment that had been sent was never even put into use. Logistical and mechanical problems, such as poor or nonexistent unloading facilities, the wrong machinery parts, and the lack of instructors or instruction manuals on the use of the equipment, all contributed to enormous waste. In many instances, railway stations resembled junkyards, with heaps of broken tractors and ploughs rusting in the sun.

Despite all the problems, there were some positive results. The first harvest in Kazakhstan, in the sum-

Threshing grain on a collective farm. After the war Stalin concentrated on developing heavy industry at the expense of agriculture. Khrushchev believed that agriculture could be rebuilt without disturbing the military-industrial complex and set out to prove it with his Virgin Lands program.

Delegates at the 20th Party Congress, February 1956, at which Khrushchev made a speech denouncing Stalin. Khrushchev skillfully undercut his Stalinist political opponents while disguising his own role in Stalin's government. More importantly, he paved the way for a period of reform and liberalization.

The simple act of an ordinary brave man is not to participate in lies, not to support false actions . . . But it is within the power of writers and artists to do much more: to defeat the lie.
—ALEXANDER SOLZHENITSYN
Russian author

mer of 1954, produced a million and a half tons of grain more than the harvest of the previous year. Khrushchev, encouraged and confident, decreed that even more land would be opened up the following year.

Khrushchev reaped the political rewards of his great gamble. By the following winter, Malenkov had lost so much power that he resigned as head of the government. In spring 1955 Ponomarenko was also sacked from his position as first secretary of the party in Kazakhstan, and Brezhnev stepped into his place. He oversaw the 1955 harvest, which turned out to be a failure because of a severe drought, but 1956 provided a bumper crop that far exceeded everyone's expectations.

Brezhnev's reward came at the 20th Party Congress in February 1956. The congress was the first one convened since Stalin's death. Brezhnev was reelected to the Central Committee and to the Presidium as an alternate member. He found himself in the same position from which he had been so abruptly demoted three years before. Brezhnev had finally made it to the inner circle of the party's elite.

But the news of Brezhnev's reinstatement was eclipsed by Khrushchev's speech to the party's Central Committee. In a frank disclosure Khrushchev denounced Stalin. He exposed the many crimes Stalin had committed against the people during his years in power and derided Stalin's "cult of personality," accusing the dead dictator of having made himself into a demigod.

The speech stunned the delegates at the Congress and set in motion a process of de-Stalinization and liberalization that was sorely needed. Khrushchev's period of reform came to be known as "the thaw." Hundreds of thousands of political prisoners languishing in labor camps were released, and many of them were rehabilitated. Censorship in the arts and literature was relaxed in the next few years, even

Romanian citizens gather for a Stalin memorial in Bucharest in March 1953. When the news of Khrushchev's speech reached the East European Soviet bloc, many people eagerly anticipated de-Stalinization in their own countries. Romania, however, continued to adhere to the Stalinist line.

to the extent that by 1962, Alexander Solzhenitsyn's story about the inhuman conditions in the labor camps, *One Day in the Life of Ivan Denisovich*, would be published in a Soviet literary magazine.

By exposing Stalin's terrible crimes, Khrushchev was able to cast a shadow on his rivals in the party, implicating them in the dead dictator's guilt. At the same time, he was able to deflect attention from his own role as one of Stalin's most loyal lieutenants.

Brezhnev benefited from his patron's new position of power. Although as a conservative apparatchik he probably did not see the need for the denunciation campaign, Brezhnev firmly backed his patron. Khrushchev was now dependent on the support structure he had set up among the party elite, for there was serious opposition to his action. Malenkov had allied himself with the Stalinist Molotov and Kaganovich, and they waited for the opportunity to bring Khrushchev down.

Unfortunately for Khrushchev, his speech resulted in immediate destabilization in some East

In Budapest, Hungary, Khrushchev's speech triggered a full-scale rebellion. In a move for Hungarian independence, Premier Imre Nagy pulled out of the Warsaw Pact Soviet defense alliance. Khrushchev ordered the revolt promptly and brutally suppressed.

European Soviet bloc countries, where people interpreted his words as permission to oust the Stalinist leaders still in power and acquire some independence from the Soviet master. In 1956 riots erupted in Poland, and the head of the Polish Communist party, Wladyslaw Gomulka, called for a program of "democratization." Revolution erupted in Hungary. The Hungarian premier, Imre Nagy, announced that his country was pulling out of the Warsaw Pact — the defense alliance between the Soviet Union and Eastern Europe — and declared Hungary's neutrality.

Khrushchev came under fierce attack from the Stalinist faction in the Presidium for the consequences of his denouncement speech and had to act decisively. The Soviet Union sent tanks and troops into Hungary and brutally suppressed the revolution. Hundreds of Hungarians were executed, including Nagy. Another puppet leader, János Kádár, was installed.

As the Central Committee secretary who dealt with foreign Communist parties, Brezhnev probably had a hand in the decision to invade Hungary. Certainly, one of his future protégés, Yuri Vladimirovich Andropov, as Soviet ambassador to Hungary, was pivotal to the invasion. Some say that without Andropov it might not have succeeded. In June 1957, after a final challenge to his authority by certain Presidium members, Khrushchev emerged secure in his position as Stalin's heir. His supporters moved into the highest posts in the party and government.

During the late 1950s Brezhnev's influence expanded with each successive assignment. He dealt with some of the most important matters of national security. He was put in charge of top-secret projects involving the development of rockets, nuclear missiles, and space technology. This was a sensitive and critical post, because the sophistication of the Soviet Union's military arsenal had a direct relationship to its power and foreign policy status in the world arena.

Until 1960 Brezhnev supervised almost 30 missile research and development centers and production

We have been silent for 11 years. Today nothing will stop us.
—Hungarian civilian on the 1956 revolt

The first Soviet atomic power station opened in June 1954. Brezhnev supervised development programs for atomic technology and space exploration from 1956 to 1960. He used the opportunity politically to confirm and expand contacts in the military, building his own base of political support.

plants stretching across the Soviet Union from Leningrad to Novosibirsk. In 1956 Brezhnev was appointed to the management board responsible for the development of nuclear ballistic missiles. Together with Dmitri Ustinov, the minister of defense industry, and scientist Mstislav Keldysh, Brezhnev was the force behind the rapid progress made in building up the Soviet arsenal of ICBMs, intercontinental ballistic missiles. The first Soviet ICBM was successfully test-launched in the summer of 1957.

Alarming as the ICBM launch was to the rest of the world, particularly to the United States, which was engaged in its own missile program, it paled before Brezhnev's next accomplishment. On October 4, 1957, Sputnik I, the first unmanned satellite, was sent into space. Brezhnev had overseen the project's development. His work on the space and missile programs also laid the groundwork for the first successful manned space flight, by cosmonaut Yuri Gagarin in 1961. Brezhnev was awarded the Hero of Socialist Labor for the part he played in the flight preparations.

By renewing contacts from his wartime days and building support among many of the Soviet Union's top generals, Brezhnev formed close ties with the military establishment. These alliances would later prove crucial to Brezhnev in his own bid for power.

In the late 1950s Khrushchev faced considerable criticism from the party's military leaders on his "soft" attitude toward the West, with which the Soviet leader wanted to foster better relations as part of the general thaw. As always, whenever the first secretary found himself under political fire, his protégés suffered. In May 1960 Brezhnev was appointed to the largely ornamental role of Soviet chief of state. The official title was chairman of the Presidium of the Supreme Soviet, and although lacking in real power, the post was a highly visible one. Brezhnev's official responsibilities included meeting foreign delegations, signing documents into law, and in a number of ceremonial ways, representing the Soviet state.

NOVOSTI FROM SOVFOTO

Sputnik I, the first earth satellite, was launched from the Soviet Union in October 1957. This caused a worldwide sensation as evidence of rapidly developing Soviet power and technology, and the United States escalated its own space program in order to compete with the Soviets.

Brezhnev with Prime Minister Jawaharlal Nehru in India, 1961. Brezhnev shrewdly used the largely ceremonial post of chief of state as an opportunity to expand his political prestige and international visibility while developing his abilities as a diplomat and negotiator.

Brezhnev's appointment coincided with a major foreign policy venture. In the early 1960s Soviet foreign policy experts turned their attention to the nonaligned countries of Asia and Africa. With the dissolution of many colonial empires on these two continents, the Soviets saw an opportunity to turn disaffection with the Western powers — who had been the colonialists—to their own advantage.

Brezhnev, in his role of head of state, began to court and cultivate ties with these new countries. For the first time he traveled outside the Soviet Union. In three years he managed to cover a great deal of territory. He visited several countries in Africa, including Morocco, Guinea, Ghana, Angola, and Algeria. He extended generous loans to the newly established socialist government in Mali. In Asia he made particularly favorable alliances with Indonesia and India. He also tried to undermine the influence in Asia of the Communist Chinese, with whom the Soviets had an ongoing rivalry for supremacy in the Communist world. In 1961 alone, by granting $547 million worth of aid to Third World governments, Brezhnev won many allies for the Soviet Union on his trips abroad.

Brezhnev also won the reputation in the international community of being a skilled negotiator and diplomat. His style was low-key and businesslike. He was gregarious and charming, both as a guest and as a host to foreign delegations in Moscow. Only once during this time did he lose his temper and attempt to browbeat an opponent. In 1962 Brezhnev tried to pressure Josip Broz Tito, leader of nonaligned Communist Yugoslavia, into supporting Soviet policy in Eastern Europe. Tito would not yield to the strong-arm tactic.

Although crude bullying was the exception for Brezhnev, it was becoming the norm for Khrushchev. Whereas Brezhnev was cautious and low-key, Khrushchev was forthright and overwhelming. Khrushchev's gambles in foreign policy led to some of the tensest moments between the two superpowers since World War II. Khrushchev came into sharp conflict with U.S. president John F. Kennedy on two important issues.

In 1961 Khrushchev made a proposal that called for the United States to conclude a separate peace treaty with Communist East Germany, a Soviet satellite the United States did not officially recognize. (The United States favored the reunification of East and West Germany.) The proposal also outlined a change in the status of Berlin, the former capital of Hitler's Germany. After the war Berlin was divided into zones administered by the four major allies: the United States, Great Britain, France, and the Soviet Union. Khrushchev wanted the allies to withdraw their occupation forces, thus making Berlin a neutral city. The reality, however, was that Berlin, encircled by East Germany, would fall under the Soviet sphere of influence.

As the West considered what to do, in August the borders between the two German states, which up until then had been relatively open, were suddenly closed. Overnight, the East Germans built a wall dividing East and West Berlin.

The allies refused to retreat from their section of the city. American tanks lined up on one side of the wall; Soviet tanks patrolled the other. Kennedy warned Khrushchev that the United States would

East German police on patrol, as seen through a hole in the Berlin Wall. In 1961, when the West refused to bow to Soviet pressure to sign a separate peace treaty with East Germany, the border between the two German states was closed, and the East Germans constructed the Berlin Wall, sealing off the eastern zone from West Berlin. The U.S.-Soviet confrontation over the wall ended in Khrushchev's first major defeat.

not tolerate any attempt to restrict Western access to Berlin.

After several tense weeks, Khrushchev backed down. He dropped all demands for a separate peace treaty with East Germany, but the wall stayed. It had been built to stem the flow of East Germans into the western sector of the city, and it remained the only tangible Soviet achievement from the confrontation.

Khrushchev's action was sharply criticized by the conservatives in the Kremlin. They felt that he should have continued to insist on a peace treaty with East Germany, even after the wall was built. Brezhnev, although still a loyal Khrushchev supporter, essentially agreed with them. He even continued to emphasize the need for the peace treaty long after Khrushchev had retired the theme. Although a subtle distinction, it was important, for it signaled the beginning of Brezhnev's independence from his patron — an independence that would soon turn to outright opposition.

Khrushchev's second confrontation with Kennedy occurred in October 1962 in Cuba and is known as the Cuban Missile Crisis. The two superpowers came closer to war with one another than at any other time since 1945.

The conflict centered on the deployment of offensive nuclear missiles in Cuba, a Soviet ally. Within the two years previous to the confrontation, the Soviets had built military bases on the island. American intelligence sources reported that Soviet offensive weapons, including medium-range nuclear missiles and bombers capable of carrying nuclear warheads, were being installed there.

Kennedy sternly protested to Khrushchev that he would not tolerate Soviet weapons so close to the United States. The president ordered a blockade around Cuba to prevent the delivery of any more Soviet missiles. He also sent a message to Khrushchev demanding that the existing missiles be dismantled and threatened to invade the island if these demands were not met.

When Kennedy ordered an attack on any Soviet vessel that attempted to break the blockade, Khru-

In October 1962 the United States learned that Fidel Castro (left) was allowing the installation of Soviet missiles in Cuba. U.S. president John F. Kennedy immediately demanded that Khrushchev (right) dismantle and remove the missiles. For the second time in little more than a year, the United States and the Soviet Union came perilously close to war.

shchev finally gave in and agreed to dismantle the missiles. Khrushchev suffered a major diplomatic defeat in Cuba, and the party grew more and more dissatisfied with the unpredictable first secretary. In addition to setbacks in foreign policy, Khrushchev also wreaked domestic havoc in the structure of government and the party by bringing about change in too haphazard a manner. He transferred significant economic powers from national ministers to regional officials, cutting off his support among the national ministers. He alienated the apparatchiks by abolishing the traditional "cash bonuses" handed out to party executives. Khrushchev was losing the support of more and more members of the Kremlin's ruling circle, among them his own protégés.

By the early 1960s Brezhnev had become quite powerful in his own right, and he no longer needed Khrushchev's protection. He did not suddenly break ranks with Khrushchev, but he could afford to strike a more independent posture. From June 1963 to July 1964, he carefully allied himself with Khrushchev's opposition in the Presidium — most notably, with party theoretician Mikhail Suslov. During this time Brezhnev held two jobs. While still retaining his post as Soviet head of state, he was once more reelected to the Central Committee of the Secretariat, wherein real power was vested.

Although it is not known exactly when or how the plot to oust Khrushchev first took shape, it is more than likely that Suslov was behind it. Khrushchev's foreign policy blunders, his ill-prepared schemes to restructure Soviet bureaucracy at home, and his continued use of de-Stalinization policies to consolidate his own power within the party were too much for this keeper of party orthodoxy.

The extent of Brezhnev's involvement in the coup is uncertain. It is widely believed that he did not instigate it, but was chosen by the opposition leaders as Khrushchev's successor, becoming involved only after the plan had already taken shape. Brezhnev had shown enough independence in the last few years to make him an acceptable alternative. He favored a hard-line policy in negotiations with the

EASTFOTO

Khrushchev (left) visits President Tito in Yugoslavia, August 1963. By this time, Khrushchev's foreign policy blunders and governmental reorganization schemes had alienated the top Soviet leadership. Brezhnev, confident of his own power base, joined in the plot to oust the unpredictable Khrushchev.

West, which endeared him to the military establishment. His support of the de-Stalinization campaign was only lukewarm. He wondered about the detrimental effect it had on the party's — and his own — ultimate authority.

In October 1964 Khrushchev was brought into a meeting of the Presidium and presented with an ultimatum — either he went willingly or he would be kicked out. Surrounded by the opposition, Khrushchev gave up, and he was allowed to retire on a pension. On October 15, 1964, Soviet citizens heard an announcement of Khrushchev's "request for retirement," and the subsequent election of Leonid Brezhnev as first secretary of the Communist party of the Soviet Union.

5

The Pendulum Swings Back

Since the beginning of the Soviet state in 1917, party ideology has emphasized the importance of collective leadership. The revolution, after all, had been fought to get rid of that ultimate expression of one-man rule — the tsarist monarchy. Yet each leader, from Lenin to Brezhnev, methodically disarmed his opponents in the party and secured the leadership role entirely for himself.

It was Brezhnev's turn to set the process in motion. When named first secretary in October 1964, his speeches were replete with calls for rule by the collective leadership of the party. He attacked Khrushchev, now derisively referred to as "Tsar Nikita," for having committed the unpardonable sin of creating a "cult of personality," the same accusation Khrushchev had leveled at Stalin. Brezhnev, too, while decrying Khrushchev, was slowly starting his own image-building mechanisms. He now had to accomplish quite contradictory tasks. He had to assure the traumatized party apparatchiks that he would not encroach on their privileges. At the same time, Brezhnev had to neutralize his rivals within the party leadership.

> *We were scared — really scared. We were afraid the thaw might unleash a flood.*
> —NIKITA KHRUSHCHEV explaining why Brezhnev ended the thaw

Brezhnev was named first secretary in October 1964. He was able to obtain this post because of his farsighted, behind-the-scenes political manipulation. Although he had not openly contradicted Khrushchev's policies, Brezhnev had dissented from them sufficiently to establish himself as an independent force.

TASS FROM SOVFOTO

Brezhnev was challenged by several rivals when he moved into position as Khrushchev's heir. Aleksei Kosygin (right), shown here on a state visit to India, was one of Brezhnev's most powerful adversaries. As chairman of the Council of Ministers, Kosygin essentially controlled the government apparatus.

These rivals were many. Of immediate concern were the men with whom Brezhnev shared power. In 1964 Aleksei Kosygin became chairman of the Council of Ministers — in other words, head of the government. Kosygin, uninterested in leading the party, simply wanted to run the government with as little outside interference as possible. He would challenge Brezhnev's party encroachment on the government apparatus repeatedly through the next 10 years.

Nikolai Podgorny, the person whom Khrushchev had brought to Moscow from the Ukraine and installed on the Secretariat to check Brezhnev's growing power, was still a force to be reckoned with. Podgorny favored the Khrushchevian policy of emphasis on consumer goods industry over the defense sector. Brezhnev, backed by his longtime supporters in defense and heavy industry, was able to remove Podgorny from the Secretariat in 1965, "promoting" him to chairman of the Supreme Soviet Presidium, the less influential post that he himself had held.

There were other rivals. Alexander Shelepin, an ambitious, arrogant, and extremely talented man who had been appointed by Khrushchev in 1958 to head the KGB, posed a serious threat to Brezhnev in those early days. (In the mid-1940s the NKVD had become the KGB — the Committee for State Security.) Brezhnev was able to remove him from influential positions only slowly, imperceptibly, over a number of years. It was not until 1967, in fact, that Brezhnev was able to install someone much more to his liking as KGB chief — Yuri Andropov, the Soviet ambassador to Hungary in 1956.

Brezhnev shuffled the apparatus to move his own clients into favorable positions in Moscow. Most members of Brezhnev's entourage came from his home region in the Ukraine, Dnepropetrovsk. Many associations went back to his early days as a young party bureaucrat there in the late 1930s.

Andrei Kirilenko, for example, was one of the so-called Dnieper Mafia. Brezhnev's subordinate immediately after the war and later first secretary of the Dnepropetrovsk region, Kirilenko was brought into the Central Committee in 1966, later promoted into the Politburo, and throughout the 1970s was Brezhnev's second-in-command. Other members of the "Mafia" came from other stages in Brezhnev's long career. From his wartime days, Brezhnev promoted marshals Malinovsky and Grechko. From his days at Zaporozhstal Brezhnev brought Venyamin Dymshits to Moscow; the latter was promoted four times in three years. From his Moldavian days, Brezhnev recruited Semyon Tsvigun — to whom he was related by marriage — to be deputy chairman of the KGB. He also recruited Moldavia's one-time chief of propaganda, Konstantin Chernenko, who eventually replaced Kirilenko in the late 1970s as Brezhnev's chief lieutenant.

Brezhnev's influence, naturally, extended beyond positions on the national level and into the party apparatus at republic and regional levels. In Kazakhstan, he secured the first secretaryship for his deputy from the Virgin Lands Program, Dinmukhamed Kunayev. In the Ukrainian republic organization, largely Podgorny's stronghold, Brezhnev

[Brezhnev] was less interested in initiating change than in arbitrating between diverse corporate views.
—JONATHAN STEELE
British journalist

71

promoted the interests of Vladimir Shcherbitsky, who became a member of the Politburo in 1971.

There were scores of others who benefited from Brezhnev's patronage. Indeed, Brezhnev personified and perfected the system of rewarding favorites with the tempting privileges that were sought after by all. Brezhnev consolidated his power, in effect, by buying off the apparatchiks. He bestowed jobs, *dachas* (vacation homes), and foreign trips on his subordinates. He gave them a reason to remain loyal, thus ensuring the party's control of the country and his own position as its leader.

Included among the privileged ranks of Soviet society were heads of institutes, prominent scientists and academicians, directors of theaters and film studios, and a few selected brilliant performers — such as ballet stars or opera singers — who brought positive international publicity to the Soviet Union. Under Brezhnev, this privileged Soviet class, known commonly as the *nomenklatura*, prospered.

The gulf in the standard of living between the vast majority of the population and the nomenklatura was enormously wide. Unlike ordinary Soviet citizens, people in the nomenklatura were not plagued by the acute problems of everyday living that their nonprivileged compatriots faced. They had access to better food and housing, better medical care, and better education for their children than did the average citizen.

In a country with a chronic housing shortage these nomenklatura families easily obtained spacious two- or three-bedroom flats — modest by Western standards, but luxurious by Soviet ones. They enjoyed the use of special vacation homes to which ordinary citizens had no access. Members of the nomenklatura shopped in special stores where even exotic gourmet foods, such as caviar and sturgeon, were easily obtainable. They never experienced food shortages or had to wait in long lines to buy food — common headaches for the average Soviet citizen.

What distinguished the nomenklatura from its wealthy counterparts in Western societies was that political ideology, not money, determined their standard of living. The access to special stores,

Brezhnev attempted to consolidate his power by offering privileges and material rewards to his supporters. This army officer and his wife, for example, enjoyed a shipboard honeymoon in return for supporting the party line.

dachas, and other material benefits could not be purchased, only bestowed. Only those who adhered to the correct party line would be favored. Because the party held both political and economic power in the Soviet Union, it was in the position to grant and withdraw these privileges.

Throughout his career, Brezhnev took advantage of his status and secured a much more comfortable life for himself than he possibly could have dreamed of as a small boy from a poor family in Kamenskoye. More than any other party boss, Brezhnev managed to insulate himself from knowledge of the hard economic realities of daily life for millions of Soviet citizens.

The system of state-given privileges was the perfect breeding ground for corruption. Free for the first time from Stalin's terror or Khrushchev's reorganization schemes, the nomenklatura under Brezhnev engaged in all kinds of illegal activities, such as the sale of party and government jobs, diamond and gold smuggling, bribery, and black marketeering.

The black market — the Soviet Union's illegal and vast second economy — operated in a variety of ways. All of them, however, hinged on privileges and how to use them to advantage in a society that had a scarcity of consumer goods.

For instance, permission to travel outside the Soviet Union, especially to the West, was a rare privilege granted only to people with connections. Those lucky enough to go abroad often used their trips as major business expeditions to buy Western goods such as blue jeans, cameras, tape cassette players, video recorders, and many other items. Domestic consumer goods were unavailable or of markedly inferior quality.

The resale value of these goods on the black market was often 10 times what it had been in the West. One pair of Western blue jeans, for example, could command up to 180 rubles — about $200 — in the Soviet Union. Transactions on the black market were illegal. Nevertheless, such transactions were practiced on all levels of society, especially at the higher levels.

Scandals involving corruption and bribery would be common throughout Brezhnev's 18 years as Soviet leader. Yet in 1964, Brezhnev was exactly the kind of man the party bureaucrats wanted. He was interested not only in preserving the status quo, but also favored turning back the clock to a considerable degree. All of Khrushchev's reorganization schemes were halted. The regional-level offices he had created

Brezhnev with a Chaika, the automobile of the Soviet elite. Brezhnev's passion for automobiles and his general love of luxury items were well known, and he used his privileged position to enjoy a lifestyle unknown to most Soviet citizens.

Prominent Soviet athletes were materially rewarded for winning in international competition. Here, Olympic champion Vladimir Salnikov (center) with his teammates Victor Kuznetsov (left) and Sergei Rusin wear the quintessential badge of status — Western blue jeans.

were disbanded, and the national ministries were returned to their former functions.

Brezhnev set the tone of his leadership in 1966 at the 23rd Party Congress. There, in a speech about Stalin's wartime role, Brezhnev made favorable public references to the dead dictator for the first time in a decade. On a limited scale, Stalin was being rehabilitated.

The Presidium was renamed the Politburo, the name it had under Stalin. Brezhnev changed his own title from first secretary to general secretary — Stalin's title. In time, toward the end of his life, Brezhnev was addressed as *vozhd*, a title of high stature that had previously only been used to refer to Stalin.

The swing back to a more orthodox orientation soon made itself felt on the country's cultural life and the arts. Under Khrushchev, stringent censorship had seen a certain relaxation that allowed writers and other artists to test and expand the limits of what was permissible. Censorship had not disappeared entirely, however. Indeed, during the thaw Boris Pasternak, one of the Soviet Union's greatest writers, was persecuted, and his works were placed under a total ban after he wrote his epic novel on the Russian Revolution, *Dr. Zhivago*. The winner of the 1958 Nobel Prize for Literature, Pasternak was not officially rehabilitated until 1987, when it

In 1958 Boris Pasternak was awarded the Nobel Prize for his novel on the Russian Revolution, *Dr. Zhivago*, but was harassed by the Soviet government, which had banned the work, into refusing the prize. Under Brezhnev censorship was very strict.

was announced that *Dr. Zhivago* would finally be published in the Soviet Union.

The late 1950s and early 1960s saw an increase in *samizdat*, or "self-publishing" literature, which operated outside the control of the government and was therefore illegal. Those authors who wrote works critical of the Soviet government, exposed flaws in the "perfect" socialist state, or dealt with subjects prohibited by the censors were forced to publish secretly. Samizdat authors had no access to printing presses or copy machines, all of which were controlled by the government. Manuscripts were typed or copied by hand and passed from person to person in a well-developed underground network. Samizdat journals, free from the restraints of state censorship, featured a preponderance of poetry, short stories, and essays. These works proliferated in Moscow and Leningrad and, to some extent, in other major cities of the Soviet Union.

Under Brezhnev, Khrushchev's tentative moves toward liberalization ended, and samizdat, barely a few years old, was quickly attacked by the authorities. The first overt signal that the Khrushchevian thaw was over came in 1966 when two writers, Yuli Daniel and Andrei Sinyavsky, were arrested and tried for spreading "anti-Soviet propaganda." Their real crime had been to send some of their manuscripts to the West. Sinyavsky was sentenced to seven years in prison, Daniel to five years.

Their trial was the first to be reported in depth by Western correspondents in Moscow. In addition, several of the writers' friends and acquaintances showed their support publicly by going to the courthouse every day. This open support was a new phenomenon, and it marked the beginning of the open dissident movement in the Soviet Union during Brezhnev's reign.

The seeds of the movement, of course, had been sown during the thaw. Many people had responded to Khrushchev's liberalization by beginning to question long-accepted ideas about their own society. They had begun to ask uncomfortable questions about their own recent past — the collectivization campaigns, the famines, Stalin's purges in the

1930s, and the Soviet Union's role in World War II. They made the first tentative moves to explore alternative ways of action in the cultural, economic, or political spheres.

During Brezhnev's years in power, dissidents protested censorship, religious persecution, discrimination against Jews, the Russification of ethnic minorities, the Soviet invasion of Czechoslovakia and Afghanistan, and many other issues. The dissident movement, never organized or structured along the traditional lines of an opposition party, was largely a spontaneous response by individual Soviet citizens. It was characterized by its peaceful and — according to the Soviet constitution — legal activity of asking the state to respect its own laws. At first, protests took the form of letters addressed to Brezhnev and other Kremlin leaders asking that they respect the constitutional rights to free expression. Occasionally dissidents would gather signatures on petitions protesting that someone had been illegally arrested for political reasons. They sometimes staged public protest demonstrations against acts by the Soviet government. These demonstrations never lasted more than a matter of minutes, for the KGB immediately broke them up, usually arresting the participants.

A few very vocal dissidents became well known in the West. Alexander Solzhenitsyn, for example, whose early work had been officially published under Khrushchev, was perhaps the strongest dissident voice in the early 1970s. Under Brezhnev, however, none of Solzhenitsyn's work was published in the Soviet Union. Instead he sent his novels to the West, where they quickly brought him international acclaim, and he was awarded the Nobel Prize for Literature in 1970. Solzhenitsyn's detailed chronicle of Stalin's labor camps, *The Gulag Archipelago*, finally caused his expulsion from the Soviet Union. In 1974 Solzhenitsyn, together with his young wife and two children, was expelled from the country and stripped of Soviet citizenship.

Andrei Sakharov came from the privileged class in Soviet society. He was a scientist who had been instrumental in developing the hydrogen bomb for

UPI/BETTMANN NEWSPHOTOS

During Khrushchev's "thaw" writer Alexander Solzhenitsyn's story about labor camp conditions, *One Day in the Life of Ivan Denisovich*, was published in a Soviet literary magazine. By 1974 the outspoken author had so exasperated Brezhnev that he was expelled from the Soviet Union.

the Soviet Union. Sakharov personified the democratic wing of Soviet dissent. He favored a system in which there was a place for all different opinions. His outspokenness against the persecution of dissidents was persistent and embarrassing to the Soviet government. He signed petitions, attended trials of dissidents all over the country, and published articles in samizdat and in the West. After Solzhenitsyn's expulsion, Sakharov became the best known spokesman of Soviet dissent to Westerners. As a result, he was thrown out of the Academy of Sciences (and so denied access to research facilities), stripped of all his titles and privileges, and eventually, exiled from Moscow to the city of Gorky after he protested the Soviet invasion of Afghanistan.

There were many other kinds of dissidents. Some were religious, others — especially in the non-Russian republics — were nationalist. Sometimes the two were combined, as in Lithuania, where repression of Catholicism coincided with the state's policy to eradicate Lithuanian nationalist feeling. Jews who wished to explore their heritage through religious or cultural activities or who had applied to emigrate also formed a strong dissident voice. Persecution of Jews and state-sponsored anti-Semitism increased under Brezhnev.

At the very least, dissidents lost their jobs. Ordinary workers could find no one to hire them. Party members were kicked out of the party and students were thrown out of universities. Writers were expelled from the Writers' Union — the official organization to which every Soviet author belonged — and effectively blacklisted. Academicians and professors, unable to find employment in their chosen fields, could only find work at menial occupations, such as boiler stokers and bathhouse attendants. Many were arrested and sentenced to long years in labor camps, followed by additional years of internal exile, usually in Siberia. Although there are no reliable statistics available, human-rights organizations in the West estimate that under Brezhnev there were about 10,000 political prisoners in the Soviet Union.

Repression often did not stop at the prison gates. Confinement to psychiatric hospitals was a particularly frightening development under Brezhnev. Khrushchev had first introduced this practice, stating that only someone mentally unstable would find fault with the Soviet system. In the 1970s new mental "diseases" were "discovered" by medical authorities to lend scientific authenticity to this form of punishment. During Brezhnev's years in power, it is estimated that close to 1,000 people were incarcerated in Soviet psychiatric institutions for political reasons. They were often forcibly injected with painful and debilitating drugs normally used to treat real mental illnesses. When applied to mentally healthy people, however, the drugs caused paranoia, depression, severe disorientation, and other symptoms. Many dissidents suffered permanent damage as a result of drug treatment. Soviet psychiatrists who protested the abuse of the medical profession to silence dissent, such as Dr. Anatoli Koryagin, were themselves often arrested and given very harsh sentences. Koryagin, a member of an independent group in Moscow that monitored the government's abuse of psychiatric treatment, was arrested in 1981 and sentenced to seven years in a labor camp and five years internal exile for his activity and outspokenness.

By the time Brezhnev died in 1982, he had managed to nearly cripple the dissident movement in the Soviet Union. Many dissidents were unable to withstand the repression of the state and simply ceased their activity. Others were kicked out of the country, exiled to the West. Still others gave up hope of ever changing the system and sought permission to emigrate. Many of their friends, of course, suffered far worse fates. Some had died in the camps or as a result of long years of harassment by the relentless authorities.

When Andrei Sakharov was in exile in Gorky, isolated from his friends and suffering from heart disease, he was told by the KGB physician assigned to him, "We won't let you die, but we will make you an invalid." The same could be said for what Brezhnev managed to do to a generation of Soviet dissenters.

6

Détente and the Global Battle for Peace

When Brezhnev stepped into Khrushchev's shoes in 1964, he inherited more than just the leadership of the Soviet Union. He assumed the position of leading spokesman for the Communist movement worldwide.

This was a role the Soviet Union had always presumed as its own. Fifty years after Lenin founded the first Communist state, Brezhnev discovered that this position was being seriously challenged. There were, it seemed, communists elsewhere who did not think the Soviets should claim to be the high priests of party ideology.

The most powerful of these challengers was China. Mao Zedong, ruler of the People's Republic of China since 1949, refused to bow to Soviet presumptions of superiority. After all, China's population of almost 1 billion people was 4 times that of the Soviet Union. Relations between the two countries deteriorated to such an extent that by 1969, scattered conflicts broke out along their border.

Under Josip Broz Tito, Yugoslavia managed to break away from Soviet domination immediately

> *Peace, peace, and once again peace, is our cardinal task.*
> —LEONID BREZHNEV

General Secretary Brezhnev in his study in the Kremlin. During the 1970s Brezhnev increasingly neglected domestic affairs to make his mark on the international stage. With his policies of détente and disarmament, Brezhnev hoped to promote an image of the Soviet Union as world peacemaker.

Chairman Mao Zedong of China. In the 1960s China challenged Soviet authority in the Communist world and relations between the two became so strained that open border conflicts erupted.

after World War II. While maintaining a Communist government, Tito sought to steer an independent course for Yugoslavia between the Soviet-dominated Eastern-bloc countries — Poland, Hungary, Romania, Czechoslovakia, the German Democratic Republic, and Bulgaria—and the Western democracies.

In the 1960s the Communist parties of other countries — particularly those in Western Europe — joined the challenge to the Kremlin's traditional authority. Brezhnev sought to counter this erosion of Soviet authority in the worldwide Communist movement by proposing an international conference to be held in Moscow. He invited all the Communist parties of the world — those in power, in opposition, or underground. Brezhnev wanted to reaffirm Soviet preeminence and enhance Soviet prestige internationally.

While Brezhnev was unhappy with the disenchantment of Communist parties worldwide, he became alarmed with the challenge posed by a Communist party much closer to home — in Czechoslovakia. Political developments there so threatened Brezhnev that he exerted the full might of Soviet power to counterbalance them.

Czechoslovakia, which Brezhnev had helped liberate from Nazi Germany in World War II, was late in reacting to Khrushchev's de-Stalinization policies. The Stalinist leader of the country, Antonín Novotný, had managed to resist all threats to his power even after Khrushchev was already deposed.

But by late 1967, as Czechoslovakia's economy stagnated and its intellectuals clamored for more creative freedom, Novotný finally lost power to Alexander Dubček, head of the Slovak Communist

Alexander Dubček replaced the Stalinist Antonín Novotný as leader of Czechoslovakia in 1967. In his efforts to rebuild the economy and stimulate cultural life, Dubček permitted reforms that horrified Brezhnev, who saw them as a threat to Soviet domination.

EASTFOTO

party. Brezhnev went to Prague to reassure himself that Dubček would be loyal to Moscow and protect Soviet influence in Czechoslovakia, and he returned satisfied. However, his satisfaction was short-lived. While Dubček continued to profess allegiance to the Warsaw Pact and loyalty to the Soviet Union, he embarked on a program of reform in Czechoslovakia that, in Brezhnev's eyes, threatened the very legitimacy of Communist party rule.

Shortly after coming to power in January 1968, Dubček introduced reforms that were designed to revitalize Czechoslovakia's economy and cultural life. For the first time since the end of World War II, Dubček called for non-Communists to be allowed into government posts. In addition, he proposed that censorship be lifted, so that a variety of opinions could be aired without the threat of repression. Dubček favored the investigation and exposing of Stalinist crimes in Czechoslovakia as well as the rehabilitation of their victims. Perhaps most alarming to Brezhnev, however, was a proposal for democratization within the Czechoslovak Communist party that included election by secret ballot and tenure restrictions on certain party offices. Dubček, however, did not want to overthrow Czechoslovakia's socialist system of government. What he wanted, the party leader said, was to give socialism "a human face."

For seven months — from January to July 1968 — he managed to do just that. Writers and other artists flourished; works long suppressed finally found their way into print and were quickly sold out. The momentum picked up; ordinary Czechs, participating in open debates about the party's role in their country, began to question their officials and government. This brief time of reform came to be known as the "Prague Spring."

Other Communist leaders in the Eastern bloc — Walter Ulbricht in East Germany, Wladyslaw Gomulka in Poland, and Todor Zhivkov in Bulgaria — grew increasingly uneasy with the Czechoslovak developments. They were concerned that the desire for reform would soon cross over into their countries and undermine their power. Only Tito in Yugoslavia

expressed support for Dubček's actions.

Brezhnev, too, was uneasy about the unrest in the Soviet bloc but felt reluctant to use armed force in Czechoslovakia. He waited, trying to pressure and intimidate Dubček into cracking down on the dissent. In a speech in late March 1968 Brezhnev warned the leaders in Czechoslovakia that deviation from accepted party dominance would not be tolerated. In late July 1968 Brezhnev met with the Czechoslovak leader on the Soviet-Czechoslovak border in a final attempt to bully Dubček into halting the reforms. At the same time, he sounded out his colleagues in the Soviet Politburo on how best to handle the situation. In light of the upcoming 1969 World Communist Conference, which the Soviets had worked so hard to coordinate, an invasion of a fraternal Communist country would put Brezhnev in a very awkward position.

Brezhnev, in his usual manner, wavered until he was forced to take a stand. Under intense pressure from the conservatives in the Kremlin, and receiving repeated requests from Ulbricht and Gomulka that

A bloodstained Czechoslovak flag is defiantly held up to a Soviet tank crew in Prague. Brezhnev ordered an invasion of Czechoslovakia on the night of August 20, 1968. He justified his action in the "Brezhnev Doctrine," which stated that every Communist country was obligated to halt "antisocialist degeneration" in fellow Communist nations.

the Czechoslovak movement be contained, Brezhnev finally decided to act.

On the night of August 20, 1968, Soviet tanks rolled into Czechoslovakia. Paratroopers landed at the Prague airport. Troops from the Soviet Union and other Warsaw Pact countries crossed the Czechoslovak border and occupied the country. Within days, Dubček and several of his ministers were arrested and secretly brought to Moscow. Only the unified stand of the remaining top officials of the Czechoslovak party prevented Dubček from disappearing altogether. In a rare display of resistance to Soviet might, they refused to negotiate the setting-up of a new puppet government in Czechoslovakia unless Dubček was allowed to remain its head. Although Brezhnev was forced to concede on this point, he won in the end. Dubček was sidelined from politics the following year. Prague Spring was over.

Brezhnev justified the invasion of Czechoslovakia by maintaining that the Communist system itself had been in danger of collapsing there. In September *Pravda* published what came to be called the "Brezhnev Doctrine" by Western commentators. The article stated, "Every Communist party is responsible not only to its own people, but also to all socialist countries and the world Communist movement. . . . Communists in fraternal countries could not allow themselves to remain inactive in the name of an abstract principle of sovereignty while watching one of their number fall into the process of antisocialist degeneration." This doctrine of "limited sovereignty" became one of the mainstays of Brezhnev's foreign policy.

Brezhnev's World Communist Conference was finally held in June 1969, but his goals were not achieved. Only 75 out of 111 Communist parties attended. Of the 14 ruling parties, 5 — Yugoslavia, Albania, China, North Korea, and North Vietnam — boycotted the conference. Others that did attend forced the Soviets to make certain concessions, including the publication of all conference statements and speeches, even those critical of Soviet policies, in *Pravda*. Many of these statements — such as the one given by the Romanian Communists praising

China's development of socialism — were extremely embarrassing to Brezhnev. Instead of successfully reestablishing unquestioned Soviet dominance, the conference merely underscored the growing resistance to it.

Western countries had strongly condemned the Soviet invasion of Czechoslovakia. Nevertheless, their condemnation was overshadowed by other concerns. The Czechoslovak episode did not prevent them from trying to establish friendlier ties with the Soviet Union. Brezhnev, however, demonstrated that friendlier overtures to the West, particularly to the United States, were not to be accompanied by any kind of liberalization at home. Indeed, at the same time as he was trying to convince his colleagues in the Politburo of the benefits that détente — as the gradual warming of relations between the two superpowers came to be called — would bring, Brezhnev was also promoting a hard line against dissent in Soviet society and its counterpart in the Eastern-bloc countries.

Brezhnev's moves toward détente were even accepted by the Soviet military establishment, usually a staunch opponent of any kind of relaxation of tensions with the West. In his early years in power, however, Brezhnev had allocated massive amounts of resources for the military. One of his principal achievements as leader of the Soviet Union was to bring Soviet military power up to parity with the United States. Since the end of World War II, the United States had enjoyed global military superiority, especially in nuclear weapons.

Brezhnev had chafed under this situation and was determined to change it. Consequently, between 1966 and 1970, Soviet military spending nearly doubled. The development of Soviet nuclear weapons was accelerated. Between 1964 and 1968 the number of Soviet ICBMs jumped from 190 to 860, and submarine-launched missiles rose from 29 to 120. These powerful nuclear weapons had the capability of hitting targets thousands of miles away from their launching sites in a matter of minutes. In addition, Brezhnev turned the Soviet navy into a major force, capable of being deployed not only in

We shall do our utmost to ensure that the proponents of military adventurism never catch the land of the Soviets unawares.
—LEONID BREZHNEV

A Soviet intercontinental missile is paraded through Red Square in 1965. At the same time that Brezhnev was developing and improving détente with Western nations, he was also doubling the military budget for nuclear weapons to compete with Western arms production.

the coastal waters off the Soviet Union's shores, but also around the world.

Brezhnev's accomplishments brought the Soviet Union superpower status in world politics. There were even estimates that by 1969 the Soviet Union had not only achieved military parity with the United States, but in some areas had actually surpassed it. No longer could the United States plan foreign policy without taking into consideration the Soviet Union.

So when Brezhnev approached the conservative Soviet military establishment with his plans for détente, they knew that he would not sacrifice their interests. Indeed, Brezhnev saw détente as a means of keeping Soviet military strength high.

There were many reasons why Brezhnev found détente a very attractive proposition. The Soviet economy suffered greatly because of the enormous amounts of money allocated for military purposes. Brezhnev could not afford to bolster other parts of the economy — light industry and the consumer sector — at the expense of the military. He hoped that the emphasis on arms control in détente would lead to a restriction in military spending in the United

States. It would then be much easier for the Soviet Union to maintain military might, allowing Brezhnev to develop other sectors in the Soviet economy.

Brezhnev realized that although the Soviet Union had progressed by leaps and bounds and was now a superpower, technologically it still lagged far behind the United States. He looked to détente as a means of opening up channels of trade and information between East and West, which would afford greater access to the much-needed technology, especially in computers, that the West possessed.

One of the overriding concerns in the Soviet pursuit of détente was China. By 1969 Soviet relations with its Communist neighbor had soured to the point where open border warfare had erupted. When talks began in 1970 between China and the United States to normalize diplomatic relations, the Kremlin feared its worst nightmare was about to come true. Brezhnev was afraid that friendly American relations with China would leave the Soviet Union encircled, isolated, and at a strategic disadvantage in the world arena.

Brezhnev's first real move toward détente with the West occurred in the summer of 1970, when West Germany's chancellor, Willy Brandt, came to Moscow to sign a nonaggression treaty between the two countries. The first Social Democrat to be elected chancellor in West Germany since the end of World War II, Brandt was very much in favor of better relations with his Eastern-bloc neighbors. These relations had been constantly hampered in the postwar years by the refusal of the Western allies to recognize the East German government and by the refusal of the Soviets to guarantee unimpeded access to West Berlin.

The 1970 meeting symbolized the end of the cold war between West Germany and the Soviet Union and opened the doors for a much friendlier relationship. Discussions for increased trade were begun, as were preliminary talks on the status of Berlin. Brezhnev particularly savored German recognition of the Soviet Union's postwar territorial gains in Eastern Europe. Most importantly, however, Brezhnev's meeting with Brandt paved the way

> *[H]e hopes to go down in the history books as the man who made peace with Germany.*
> —Soviet editor

for détente with the United States.

During the early 1970s, as he championed his détente policy, Brezhnev engaged in a whirl of talks, negotiations, and summit meetings with Western leaders. In September 1971 Brandt went to Moscow for security talks, and the following month Brezhnev traveled to France to meet with President Georges Pompidou. Throughout early 1972 the general secretary worked on building up support in the Kremlin for a summit meeting with U.S. president Richard M. Nixon.

But Brezhnev did not confine himself to leaders of state. He brought his détente message to prominent politicians, business leaders, and journalists in each country. In nationally televised speeches in West Germany and, later, the United States, he spoke to millions of ordinary citizens and stressed the need to cease cold-war rhetoric, halt the nuclear arms race, and build stable relations for peace.

In May 1972 Richard Nixon met with the general secretary in Moscow. Their most important achievement at this meeting was the signing of the Strategic Arms Limitations Talks Interim Agreement on Offensive Systems (SALT I). In this treaty, the

Brezhnev hosts a Kremlin reception for U.S. president Richard M. Nixon in May 1972. Their summit talks led to the SALT I nuclear disarmament agreements.

TASS FROM SOVFOTO

United States and the Soviet Union agreed to limit the number of different kinds of nuclear weapons in their arsenals. The Soviet Union was limited to no more than 1,618 ICBMs, for example, while the United States was allowed no more than 1,054. A ceiling of 200 antiballistic missiles (ABMs) — defensive weapons designed to locate and destroy incoming ICBMs—was set for both countries.

Brezhnev relished his role as diplomat and international statesman. He did his best to project a genial and warm image when he went abroad. During his May 1973 visit to the United States he shed the dour, formal demeanor that all Communist party officials maintained with their own people. He bantered with reporters, displayed an affinity for dirty jokes, and even gave cowboy television-star Chuck Connors a great Russian bear hug during a visit to California. President Nixon, while not particularly charmed by Brezhnev's earthy and gregarious personality, was impressed by his practical political side. Nixon also was looking for a way to deflect attention from the disastrous Vietnam War and the growing Watergate scandal, which threatened his administration, and Brezhnev's trip received a great deal of media coverage.

Arms negotiations between the Soviet Union and the United States continued throughout the 1970s, but it became harder for both sides to come to terms. Other political events were severely undermining the détente process, and hopes for friendlier relations were dimming.

One of the biggest areas of contention lay in increased trade between the two superpowers. American businessmen were very eager for the opportunities that the Soviet market offered, but Brezhnev wanted more than their investments. He wanted the United States to grant the Soviet Union most-favored nation status, a provision that would ensure the Soviets automatic tariff reductions and other trade advantages.

Trade agreements with the Soviet Union have to be ratified by the U.S. Congress. Senator Henry Jackson wanted trade with the Soviet Union to be contingent on Soviet observance of basic human

> *Russia is inextricably woven into the history of Europe — not only as an adversary and danger but also as a partner — historical, political, cultural, and economic.*
> —WILLY BRANDT
> German chancellor

U.S. secretary of State Henry Kissinger, Brezhnev, U.S. president Gerald Ford, and Soviet Foreign Minister Andrei Gromyko meet in Helsinki, Finland. There, Brezhnev achieved Western recognition of Soviet postwar territorial claims. The Helsinki Accord represented the zenith of détente between the Soviet Union and the United States.

rights. Jackson attached amendments to trade agreements that called for denying most-favored nation status to any Communist country that prohibited its citizens from emigrating or assessed exorbitantly high exit duties.

The Soviet Union, which had closed its borders in 1917, was guilty of both practices. In the early 1970s there had been some emigration of Soviet Jews, and Jackson wanted to ensure that this would continue unhampered. Brezhnev, on the other hand, balked at such concerns, considering them inappropriate American meddling in domestic Soviet affairs. Although the general secretary never signed any formal promise, by the time he died, nearly 265,000 Soviet Jews had been allowed to leave the country, along with 75,000 ethnic Germans and 25,000 Armenians. Most of these emigrés eventually settled in Israel or the United States.

The harassment of Soviet citizens who applied to emigrate, however, did not cease. Applications to leave were begrudgingly granted by the Soviet authorities. Some people waited years before permission was given; others never received permission at all. In addition, applicants waiting to leave were soon made into outcasts in Soviet society.

Before détente began to completely unravel, Brezhnev managed to negotiate an important treaty, called the Helsinki Accord. The participants at the Helsinki Conference (officially, the Conference on Security and Cooperation in Europe) in July 1975 were the Soviet Union, the United States, and most of the European states. In a major diplomatic victory for Brezhnev, the agreement gave the Soviet Union de facto recognition of Soviet territorial gains in Europe as a result of World War II. The accord also contained a number of clauses on human rights, including freedom of speech, conscience, and movement. It called for a freer exchange of ideas and information between East and West, with special attention given to reuniting families separated by the Iron Curtain. All the signatory countries, including the Soviet Union, agreed to honor these clauses. Signed by 35 countries in July 1975 in Helsinki, Finland, the accord was, in effect, the peace treaty that Khrushchev had wanted so much and never saw.

Thirty years after the war ended, Brezhnev succeeded where his predecessor had failed. The Helsinki treaty was his moment of triumph — the culmination and decisive validation of his détente policy, and yet the agreement would end by revealing the hypocrisy of the Soviet leader. While Brezhnev trumpeted portions of the Helsinki agreement containing the concessions from the West on Soviet territorial gains, he ignored the humanitarian clauses. The double standard soon became apparent. When the full text of the Helsinki Accord was published on August 2, 1975, in *Pravda* and *Izvestiya*, Soviet dissidents read the portions pertaining to human rights, and spontaneously, independent groups sprang up around the country to monitor actual compliance by the state with these clauses. The first group originated in Moscow, and within a year, there were Helsinki Monitoring

Fragile though it may turn out to be, détente will go down as one of Brezhnev's most impressive successes.
—JONATHAN STEELE
British journalist

Groups in the Ukraine, Lithuania, Georgia, and Armenia.

Brezhnev had no intention of honoring the humanitarian clauses, but conscious of international publicity, he ordered no arrests of the Helsinki Monitoring Group members until 1977. That year the KGB began a crackdown, and three members of the Moscow group — including Jewish dissident Anatoly Shcharansky and physicist Yuri Orlov — were arrested. Members of the other groups were also picked up. Many, such as Shcharansky, were sentenced to long years in prison.

In the next few years the KGB kept up steady pressure on the human-rights activists. The intimidation of the Helsinki Monitoring Groups increased. Some members were frightened into ceasing their activity; others were exiled from the country and stripped of their Soviet citizenship. The groups continued to operate under repressive conditions, but their ability to check and report on the state's compliance with the human-rights clauses was even-

Protesters hold up posters of dissident Anatoly Shcharansky in a New York demonstration, 1978. Shcharansky, a member of the Moscow group monitoring Soviet compliance with the human-rights clauses of the Helsinki Accord, was arrested in 1977 and became an internationally recognized symbol of Soviet Jewish dissent.

AP/WIDE WORLD PHOTOS

tually crippled. The Moscow group held out the longest, but in 1982 it finally disbanded.

The last effort to salvage détente came with the SALT II agreement of June 1979. In SALT I, there had been no provisions on newer generations of nuclear arms, and both the United States and the Soviet Union had continued to develop and deploy more sophisticated weapons, making the old ICBMs and ABMs obsolete. To remedy this, talks for SALT II had begun as early as November 1974 between Brezhnev and U.S. president Gerald Ford. They stalled, however, when Jimmy Carter, who took office in 1977, called for more drastic arms cuts and stricter observation of human rights in the Soviet Union. After two years of negotiations, Brezhnev and Carter finally met at Vienna for the SALT II

U.S. president Jimmy Carter and Brezhnev outside the U.S. Embassy in Vienna, Austria, June 1979, where they signed the SALT II disarmament treaty. It never went into effect because of U.S. protests against the Soviet invasion of Afghanistan.

treaty, which set limits on the number of nuclear warheads and missiles and restricted work on new missiles. It also forbade the deployment of certain long-range cruise missiles. SALT II, however, was never ratified by the U.S. Congress, which shelved the treaty in protest over the latest act of Soviet aggression.

By the late 1970s the Soviet Union had scored many successes in helping to establish pro-Soviet governments globally, particularly in Third World countries including Angola, Vietnam, Laos, Cambodia, Mozambique, and Ethiopia. Such developments were viewed with increasing alarm in Western capitals. The Soviet invasion of Afghanistan in 1979, however, turned that alarm into outright anger.

Bordered on the west by Iran, on the south and east by Pakistan, and on the north by the Soviet Union, Afghanistan was for centuries the land route used to link the Middle East with Asia. Control of Afghanistan would afford the Soviet Union a much stronger position in promoting Soviet interests in that strategically important part of the world.

In 1978 one of the two rival factions of the country's tiny Communist party, the People's Democratic Party of Afghanistan (PDPA), staged a successful coup and came to power. The new regime, headed by Hafizullah Amin of the Khalq faction of the PDPA, was in an extraordinarily tenuous position; they were threatened by both the majority of the Afghan people, who were practicing Muslims and, therefore, anti-Communist, as well as by the rival Afghan Communist faction, the Parcham.

Throughout 1978 and 1979, Brezhnev, concerned only that Communists remain in power, committed substantial military support to Amin. He eventually determined that it would be more beneficial for Soviet interests to back the rival Communist faction, Parcham, whose leader was Babrak Karmal.

In late December 1979, close to 100,000 Soviet troops invaded Afghanistan. Airborne troops landed in the capital, Kabul, and quickly took control of the presidential palace and the radio and television stations. Amin was summarily deposed, executed, and replaced by Karmal. A "pacification" campaign, designed to wipe out the widespread resistance to the Soviet-backed Parcham, was then instigated throughout the country. Almost 2 million of the country's population of 15 million people fled their homes, and many settled in refugee camps along the Pakistani border. They brought with them reports of atrocities committed by Soviet soldiers as well as the Parcham secret police, called the *Khad.*

International outcry against the Soviet invasion was instant and almost unanimous. In January 1980 the United Nations General Assembly passed a resolution — by an overwhelming 104 votes to 18 — calling for withdrawal of Soviet troops from the country. The invasion buried détente. Arms negotiations were abruptly ended, President Carter cut American grain sales to the Soviet Union almost in half, and the United States led a boycott of the 1980 Olympic Games in Moscow.

Seven years after Brezhnev ordered the invasion of Afghanistan, and four years after his death, the country still was not "pacified." The Soviet Union had not expected such fierce resistance from the Afghan population. The *mujahedin*, Afghanistan's

[Russian leaders] crave to be respected as equals.
—RICHARD NIXON
U.S. president, 1969–74

In 1979 the Soviet Union invaded Afghanistan, an act that outraged the West. Brezhnev's bid to control Afghanistan, which was strategically extremely important in the volatile Middle East, was formally condemned twice by the UN and marked the end of détente.

guerrilla fighters, were able to inflict such massive casualties on Soviet troops that by 1986, Soviet leaders began to discuss the possibility of partial withdrawal from the country. Brezhnev would not live long enough to see the failure of his Afghanistan venture, and his last years were plagued by another major crisis in the Soviet bloc.

Born in the shipyard of the Baltic port of Gdansk, *Solidarność* — Solidarity — was the first union in Poland free of government control since the end of World War II. In a matter of months, it grew to almost 10 million members, gaining momentum, it seemed, by the hour.

Although its leaders stressed that it was only a union — not a political party — Solidarity's success in uniting both Poland's workers and intellectuals posed a clear threat to the ruling Communist party, the Polish United Workers' party (PZPR). Solidarity came to embody the Polish resentment of Soviet political and economic domination. As the Polish government was forced to grant Solidarity more and more concessions, guaranteeing its independent bargaining role, the Kremlin once again geared up for a showdown in Eastern Europe.

It appeared likely that the experience with Czechoslovakia a dozen years earlier would repeat itself. Brezhnev, invoking the doctrine of limited sovereignty, told the 26th Soviet Party Congress, "We will

Demonstrators for Solidarity in Warsaw, Poland. As a trade union, Solidarity was able to mobilize workers on an economic basis, thus sidestepping many of the Soviet party prohibitions against political dissidence. The Soviets promptly took steps to suppress the independent union.

not abandon fraternal, socialist Poland in its hour of need. We will stand by it." The Soviet Union was prepared to answer the "invitation" issued by the beleaguered Polish Communist party. Brezhnev backed his assurances with some 30 Soviet divisions, poised along the Polish-Soviet border, ready to invade.

This time, however, the invasion did not take place. Fearing a mass uprising if the Soviets invaded, Poland's government leaders bargained with Moscow for time, promising to take care of Solidarity themselves. A Polish general, Wojciech Jaruzelski, was appointed leader. In December 1981, less than a year and a half after Solidarity's birth, he declared martial law throughout the country.

Solidarity was banned. Thousands of people, including the trade union's major activists and leader Lech Walesa, were arrested. The Polish government slowly began a program to reestablish control of the country, and for millions of Poles hopes for more autonomy in their daily lives were thwarted once again. Yet as long as Soviet authority in Eastern Europe was intact, Brezhnev remained unconcerned with the wishes of those millions.

Brezhnev (left) and General Wojciech Jaruzelski review honor guards at Moscow's airport in 1982. The appointment of Jaruzelski, the imposition of martial law, and the subsequent elimination of Solidarity as a legal union was the price Polish leaders had to pay to avert a full-scale Soviet invasion.

7

Aging Leader, Changing World

Brezhnev died of a heart attack on November 10, 1982, one month short of his 76th birthday. He had been leader of the Soviet Union for 18 years, longer than anyone except Stalin. Speculation about the precarious state of his health had been going on since 1975, when he first suffered a major illness and disappeared from public view for several months. Newspapers in the West periodically announced Brezhnev's imminent death and listed his possible replacements. Soviet newspapers, of course, refrained from such speculation. They never even mentioned that the general secretary was sick.

Brezhnev never announced his own choice for successor. No one dared to suggest to the dying leader that he should think about who was to come after him.

The problem of succession was very serious, for there are no proper mechanisms in the Soviet system for choosing new leaders. When a change of leadership is imminent, nothing on the surface ever indicates it, but there are many behind-the-scenes maneuverings and political intrigues. All power struggles occur in disguised and oblique ways.

[W]ho will cry when Leonid Ilyich Brezhnev passes from the political stage?
—JOHN DORNBERG
Brezhnev biographer

Brezhnev with his great-granddaughter Galya at his vacation home in the Crimea. During the last few years of his rule, Brezhnev concentrated on enjoying the privileges his status allowed him to claim, ignoring the mounting corruption in his government.

TASS FROM SOVFOTO

101

Brezhnev's 1982 funeral procession in Red Square. In 1981, when Brezhnev was out of the public eye for a period of months, rumors circulated that he was in fact already dead and that this information was being suppressed. American humor magazines mockingly claimed that he had been sighted in a McDonald's restaurant in Ohio.

Brezhnev, though, did have his favorites. For much of his 18-year tenure, his second-in-command had been Andrei Kirilenko. Kirilenko, however, was unexpectedly sidestepped and replaced by Konstantin Chernenko in 1979, whose association with Brezhnev had begun 30 years earlier in Moldavia. During the last three years of Brezhnev's life, Chernenko was in charge of most administrative affairs in the Kremlin. In his later years Brezhnev worked only a few hours a day and never at night or on weekends. In the summers he took long, two-month vacations at his villa in the Crimea, while Chernenko minded the shop in Moscow.

Brezhnev abhorred change. He liked the familiar and the routine. These were the precise qualities that had made him so attractive to his party colleagues when he was chosen as chief in 1964. After Stalin's terror campaign and Khrushchev's unfocused reforms, the party apparatchiks wanted only stability. Brezhnev, the perfect apparatchik, ruled by consensus, balancing the various interest and power groups within the party bureaucracy. His penchant for stability, however, eventually turned into simple inertia. His style fostered a content and corrupt class of privileged bureaucrats who happily lined their own pockets without a thought for the overall good of the country. Secure and protected, they saw no reason to change, and every reason to keep things as they were.

During Brezhnev's last years, Soviet society was marked by a pervasive sense of cynicism and futility as people realized that the only way to get anything accomplished was through bribery and corruption. Anyone could be bought and everything had its price — from a passing grade on an entrance examination at a prestigious university, to a lucrative party post in a popular resort region, to a much sought-after trip to the West.

If Brezhnev was unwilling to think about a successor, so, too, were those at the top with him. They had all fought long and hard to reach their privileged positions, and they hung on to them tenaciously. The centers of power and authority — the Politburo and the Central Committee — suffered from a lack of young men and new ideas. All of Brezhnev's colleagues were as old as he. In 1980 more than half of the Politburo members were older than 70. Only one new man was added to it that year — Mikhail Gorbachev. At 49, he was the youngest member of the group.

The country, too, was stagnating. In 1982 the

> *Brezhnev defined his role as a consensus builder who would not confront, or radically deprive, major institutional interests.*
> —GEORGE W. BRESLAUER
> U.S. political scientist

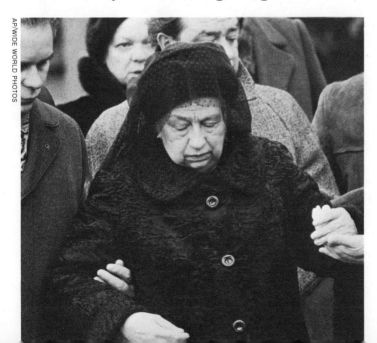

Brezhnev's wife, Viktoriya, in mourning. Married to the Soviet leader for 47 years, Viktoriya was never a visible contributor to her husband's administration. Brezhnev took care to keep her in the background.

Konstantin Chernenko (center), a longtime supporter of Brezhnev, became second in command in 1979.

Soviet economy grew by only 2 percent and had a massive foreign debt. Agriculture continued to be one of the most troubled sectors of the Soviet economy. In fact, in 1982, after three consecutive bad harvests the Soviet Union experienced the worst harvest it had seen in years. Although Brezhnev had begun to import grain from the West during détente — 43 million metric tons in 1981 alone — it was not enough to feed the Soviet people. During his last years, there was food rationing in many Soviet urban centers.

Brezhnev was guilty of fostering his own "cult of personality" with as much gusto and enthusiasm as Stalin and Khrushchev had done. His picture hung everywhere. Newspaper articles, scholarly dissertations, speeches by party bureaucrats — all contained tributes to and inspirational quotes from the general secretary. He was lauded as a political genius, a military strategist, and even a literary giant. Nine volumes of Brezhnev's collected works and three memoirs were published. The memoirs embellished his role as a political officer during World War II, in the industrial reconstruction program immediately after the war, and in the Virgin Lands program in the 1950s. For these works, he was awarded the Lenin Prize for Literature, despite his rather mediocre literary talents.

Brezhnev accumulated more awards and medals than even Stalin and Khrushchev. In 1979 he already had more than 60 military honors, including marshal of the Soviet Union. (Marshal Zhukov, a much-decorated World War II general, sported only 46.) Brezhnev had six Orders of Lenin, two orders of the October Revolution, two Orders of the Red Banner of Labor, was three times a Hero of Socialist Labor, and two times a Hero of the Soviet Union.

The general secretary openly flaunted his privileges. His fleet of expensive foreign cars was legendary. His custom-tailored suits were noticed even by Western correspondents. His penchant for hunting, soccer, and fast driving showed him to be more at home as a landed country squire than a leader of state. Showing himself a consummate materialist, Brezhnev liked the trappings that power could buy.

His family, of course, shared in the privileges. A series of scandals involving Brezhnev's family further alienated the Soviet people from a leader who, they felt, had already lost touch with the realities of Soviet life. Brezhnev's son, Yuri, who owed his position as a deputy foreign trade minister entirely to his father's patronage, had a well-known problem with alcoholism.

Brezhnev's daughter, Galina, was a flamboyant and colorful personality. She kept the gossip mills in Moscow regularly churning with news of her many love affairs. Galina favored the world of the circus — a taste she picked up from Brezhnev, who liked to visit them himself. Many of her lovers were circus performers. Her first husband was a juggler, her second an economist. She was also involved for a time with Maris Liepa, a Latvian ballet dancer.

Her third husband, Yuri Churbanov, was a lieutenant colonel in the uniformed militia. Brezhnev, relieved that Churbanov was not as flamboyant as Galina's usual partners, promptly promoted him to first deputy minister of the interior soon after their marriage. Marriage did not keep Galina away from the circus, however. She soon became involved with a tall, handsome man named Boris Buryata, nick-

> *On the base of the unfolding situation in the economy there emerged many negative phenomena of a social and spiritual moral order.*
> —commentary in *Pravda* on Soviet society during Brezhnev's last years

Poster of Brezhnev in downtown Moscow, 1982. By the last years of his life Brezhnev had fostered a cult of personality comparable to those of his predecessors. To commemorate Brezhnev's 75th birthday, articles, books, and photos were published to establish him as part of the canon of Soviet ideology and history.

Mikhail Gorbachev became general secretary in 1985. Gorbachev's age — he was the youngest Politburo member under Brezhnev — was extremely important to his success in claiming power. Gorbachev was seen as somehow untouched by the pervasive decay of Brezhnev's generation.

named Boris the Gypsy. He was often seen driving around Moscow in Galina's Mercedes-Benz. It was Boris's arrest for diamond smuggling that signaled the beginning of a sustained attack on Brezhnev's power bases in 1982.

It was rumored that Buryata's arrest brought on an irreconcilable confrontation between Brezhnev's KGB crony, Semyon Tsvigun, who wanted to hush up the affair, and the Politburo's unofficial second secretary, Mikhail Suslov. Suslov, still the party's leading theoretician, was ruthless, but incorruptible. He personally never stood for a breach of party discipline and duty. Within days, both men were dead. Tsvigun, it was rumoured, killed himself, unable to reconcile his duties as a KGB official and his loyalty to protect the Brezhnev clan. Suslov, already 79 years old, reportedly was so upset by the confrontation that he suffered a stroke, and on January 25, 1982, died as a result.

Suslov's death marked the end of an era, and was the turning point in Brezhnev's fortunes. A member of the Politburo since 1952, Suslov was the high priest of the party orthodoxy. He was a rigid ideologue, able to survive the many Kremlin intrigues because he never had any ambition to be Soviet leader himself. Yet he was known as the Kremlin's kingmaker — without Suslov's backing, Brezhnev would never have become the country's leader.

From that point on, the fight for Brezhnev's position took on new and aggressive dimensions. Throughout that last year, not only were several of his corrupt cronies arrested, but he, too, became the target of indirect, yet very pointed, attacks.

Although the disguised campaign by his ambitious Politburo colleagues to discredit him began only in the last year of his life, Brezhnev for years had been the butt of Soviet jokes and stories. Soviet citizens poked fun at his well-known vanity, his increasing feeblemindedness, and his limited intellectual abilities. As Brezhnev chose to ignore the problems, scandals, and general political decay in his government, the people responded with increasingly barbed jokes. "Stalin, Khrushchev and Brezhnev were on a train to communism when it suddenly stopped. When the train did not go again, Stalin ordered the crew to be taken out and shot. That done, the train still did not move. So Khrushchev ordered the crew rehabilitated posthumously. Still, the train did not go. So Stalin and Khrushchev turned to Brezhnev. He pulled down the shades and said, 'Now let's pretend the train is moving.' "

Still, Brezhnev succeeded in one way where both his predecessors, Stalin and Khrushchev, failed. He was not officially "forgotten." When he died, his party colleagues buried him with the degree of pomp befitting a Soviet leader. Although his portraits were taken down, and the adulatory, effusive tributes ceased, he was not entirely written out of the history books as Stalin and Khrushchev had been.

Brezhnev was essentially a bureaucrat whose talents lay in manipulating the party organization to achieve his goals. His greatest contribution to the Soviet people was that he offered them a period of peace and relative stability. Attacks against freedom, reform, and change, however, were the prices they paid for this stability. The party's totalitarian control remained intact not only in the Soviet Union but throughout the Soviet bloc. Any attempt at greater autonomy was swiftly stifled, as the Czechs, Poles, and Soviet dissidents painfully learned.

Although genuinely interested in securing peace, Brezhnev was not willing to sacrifice massive Soviet military buildup or yield superiority to the United States in nuclear arms. Nor did he respect the sovereignty of other nations — such as Afghanistan — when Soviet influence was at stake. Détente, ultimately, was Brezhnev's greatest triumph in foreign policy, but it was also his greatest disappointment when it failed to establish a favorable economic climate within the Soviet Union.

Leningrad poet Joseph Brodsky, exiled to the West in 1972, best summed up Brezhnev's legacy in his 1982 "Epitaph to a Tyrant":

> He could have killed more
> than he could have fed
> but chose to do neither. By falling dead
> he leaves a vacuum and the black Rolls-Royce
> to one of the boys who will make the choice.

Brezhnev has been treated by Soviet critics as a conservative figure, neither as bad nor as good as he could have been. His principal achievement remains his success in the development of détente, hence the association of his image with the message of "Peace" in this poster.

Further Reading

Alexeyeva, Ludmilla. *Soviet Dissent: Contemporary Movements for National, Religious, and Human Rights.* Middletown, CT: Wesleyan University Press, 1985.

Binyon, Michael. *Life in Russia.* New York: Pantheon, 1983.

Butson, Thomas G. *Mikhail Gorbachev.* New York: Chelsea House, 1987.

Dornberg, John. *Brezhnev: The Masks of Power.* New York: Basic Books, 1974.

Gelman, Harry. *The Brezhnev Politburo and the Decline of Detente.* Ithaca: Cornell University Press, 1984.

Murphy, Paul. *Brezhnev: Soviet Politician.* Jefferson, NC: McFarland, 1981.

Smith, Hedrick. *The Russians.* New York: Quadrangle, 1976.

Chronology

Dec. 19, 1906	Born Leonid Ilich Brezhnev in Kamenskoye, Ukraine
Nov. 7, 1917	Lenin leads Bolsheviks in Russian Revolution
1918–20	Civil war rages
1923	Brezhnev joins Komsomol, the Young Communist League
1924	Stalin emerges as leader of Soviet Union after Lenin's death
1928	Brezhnev marries Viktoriya Petrovna; appointed deputy chief of Sverdlovsk province
1929	Stalin institutes collectivization program
1931	Brezhnev joins the Communist party
1933	Becomes director of Metallurgical Institute Workers' Faculty in Kamenskoye
1934–38	Stalin purges the Communist party
June 22, 1941	Nazi Germany invades the Soviet Union
1941–44	Brezhnev serves in the 18th Army as political commissar
1946	Manages postwar economic reconstruction of Zaporozhye region
1953	Khrushchev becomes first secretary
1954–56	Brezhnev implements Khrushchev's Virgin Lands program in Kazakhstan
1956–60	Supervises development of nuclear missile and space programs
1960–63	Travels widely outside the Soviet Union as chief of state, gaining diplomatic experience
Oct. 1964	Khrushchev ousted; Brezhnev chosen first secretary (general secretary)
1966	Writers Sinyavsky and Daniel convicted in start of Brezhnev's crackdown on dissidents
Aug. 20–21, 1968	Brezhnev orders invasion of Czechoslovakia to restore Soviet authority
Sept. 1968	Announces doctrine of "limited sovereignty" for Eastern-bloc nations
Aug. 1970	Signs treaty with West German chancellor Willy Brandt, initiating détente
May 1972	Signs SALT I nuclear disarmament agreement with U.S. president Richard Nixon
July 1975	Negotiates Helsinki Accord, international agreement confirming Soviet territorial gains from World War II
Dec. 1979	Orders invasion of Afghanistan
Aug. 1980	Massive strikes led by Solidarity convulse Poland
Dec. 13, 1981	Polish leader Wojciech Jaruzelski declares martial law; Solidarity is banned
Nov. 10, 1982	Brezhnev dies, aged 75, of a heart attack

Index

Ina L. Navazelskis is a specialist in Eastern European affairs. A graduate of the London School of Economics and the Columbia University School of Journalism, she has published numerous articles and has been active internationally in the cause of human rights. She has traveled extensively in Eastern Europe and the Soviet Union.

Arthur M. Schlesinger, jr., taught history at Harvard for many years and is currently Albert Schweitzer Professor of the Humanities at City University of New York. He is the author of numerous highly praised works in American history and has twice been awarded the Pulitzer Prize. He served in the White House as special assistant to Presidents Kennedy and Johnson.

17.95